W9-BWX-004

"Getting parents connected to . . . their schools is tougher than ever. This guidebook is a great tool for making sense of it all. Armed with a good understanding of how schools work, parents can make an even bigger difference in their kids' schools and educational successes."
—Tim Sullivan, Founder, PTO Today, Inc.

"There are few bigger mysteries than what goes on in today's classrooms. Molland guides parents through the schoolhouse doors in a manner that is at once clear, sage, and reassuring."
—Linda Perlstein, Author of *Tested: One American School Struggles to Make the Grade*

"All the information a parent could use, from the first day and for years to come."
—Richard Eyster, Principal, Packer Collegiate Institute

"A contemporary and timely book that leads parents, educators, and the community through the labyrinth of public education in a format and language that is easy to use and understand. A resource guide that anyone concerned about public education should have."
—Arnold F. Fege, Director of Public Engagement and Advocacy, Public Education Network

Straight Talk About Schools Today

101 Q&As for Parents

Understand the System and Help Your Child Succeed

Judy Molland, B.A. Hons., Dip. Ed.

free spirit
PUBLiSHiNG®

Meeting kids'
social & emotional
needs since 1983

Library of Congress Cataloging-in-Publication Data
Molland, Judy.
    Straight talk about schools today : understand the system and help your child succeed / Judy Molland.
        p. cm.
    ISBN-13: 978-1-57542-219-0
    ISBN-10: 1-57542-219-0
1. Public schools—United States. 2. School choice—United States. 3. Academic achievement—United States. 4. Education, Elementary—Parent participation—United States. I. Title.
    LA219.M65 2007
    371.010973—dc22   2006100713

At the time of this book's publication, all facts and figures cited are the most current available. All telephone numbers, addresses, and Web site URLs are accurate and active; all publications, organizations, Web sites, and other resources exist as described in this book; and all have been verified as of February 2007. The author and Free Spirit Publishing make no warranty or guarantee concerning the information and materials given out by organizations or content found at Web sites, and we are not responsible for any changes that occur after this book's publication. If you find an error or believe that a resource listed here is not as described, please contact Free Spirit Publishing. Parents, teachers, and other adults: We strongly urge you to monitor children's use of the Internet.

The people depicted on the cover and inside the book are models and are used for illustrative purposes only. The names of the young people quoted in the book have been changed to protect their privacy.

Information about bullying on pages 81–84 includes adapted material from "Together We Can Be Bully Free: A Mini-Guide for Parents" by Allan L. Beane (Minneapolis: Free Spirit Publishing, 2004), and is used with permission of the publisher.

Editors: James Bitney and Marjorie Lisovskis
Cover design: Marieka Heinlen
Interior design: Percolator
Editorial assistant: Carla Valadez

10 9 8 7 6 5 4 3 2 1
Printed in the United States of America

Free Spirit Publishing Inc.
217 Fifth Avenue North, Suite 200
Minneapolis, MN 55401-1299
(612) 338-2068
help4kids@freespirit.com
www.freespirit.com

As a member of the Green Press Initiative, Free Spirit Publishing is committed to the three Rs: Reduce, Reuse, Recycle. Whenever possible, we print our books on recycled paper containing a minimum of 30% post-consumer waste. At Free Spirit it's our goal to nurture not only children, but nature too!

green press INITIATIVE

This book is dedicated to my son Will, who has brought so much joy to my life. Every parent should be so lucky.

ACKNOWLEDGMENTS

My thanks go out first to all the parents, teachers, and students who have shared their stories with me. It's one of the secrets that, as an education reporter, I have kept to myself: my own passion for teaching and learning is rekindled every day by the passion and dedication I feel from those I interview. They inspire me and make me love my job.

I'm grateful, too, for the many friends and colleagues who have supported me in this project; in particular, Wendy Belcher, Kathy Emery, Freda Greene, Martha Jackson, Paul McLaughlin, Mary Mihaly, Ellen Nordberg, Irene O'Garden, Laurie Scheer, Janet Simms, Matthew Simms, and Caroline Smith. Then there are the professionals—writers and editors—who have guided me along the way. To Jack Bierman, Diane Debrovner, Bill Lindsay, Christina Elston Sparrow, Lyn Stimer, Dana Truby, and Deirdre Wilson, a huge thank you. Thanks to Judy Galbraith for giving me the opportunity to realize my dream and to my editors at Free Spirit, Margie Lisovskis and Jim Bitney, for their expertise, hard work, and cheerful advice. Finally I thank my husband Joe for providing love, support, technical advice, dinners, and a sense of humor, and for believing in this project from the beginning.

CONTENTS

Chapter 3: Getting Started in Kindergarten 41

Chapter 4: Changing Schools 56

Chapter 5: Making the Most of the School Year 64

Chapter 6: The Connected Classroom and the Wired School 89

Chapter 7: Understanding Reporting Systems and Communication Tools 104

INTRODUCTION

The idea for *Straight Talk About Schools Today* grew out of my work as the teaching expert on the "Ask the Teacher" feature of Education.com, Vivendi Universal's education Web site:

- "My child is in sixth grade for the second time, and his grades are very low. What can I do to help him?"
- "My daughter will be starting kindergarten in the fall. How do I know if she's ready?"
- "Why do teachers give out homework?"
- "My third-grade son has told me that the book his teacher is reading is too scary. He has tried plugging his ears, but he still hears the story. What should I do?"
- "There are so many options in my district—charter schools, magnet schools, vouchers . . . how do I choose the right school for my daughter?"
- "Can I request a particular teacher, and is that a good idea?"
- "How should my child be using a computer at school?"
- "What's in my child's permanent record? Can I see it?"
- "Why does my child have to take standardized tests? What do the scores mean, and how are they used?"

Every day I received dozens of questions like these from parents asking for basic information on how their child's school operates and where to turn if they had a problem. As I answered each question, I searched for a book I could refer parents to for more information, but could find none. The education shelves of bookstores were filled with volumes discussing curriculum, detailing what a third, fourth, or fifth grader should know, weighing the pros and cons of homeschooling, or dissecting the history of education over the twentieth century—all important topics, but less than help-ful for parents who have received a letter stating that their child's school has been labeled "in need of improvement" and who have no idea what that means. And so the idea for *Straight Talk About Schools Today* was born. My goal in writing it has been to provide a guidebook to "the system" along with answers to the many ques-tions parents have asked me about the workings of their children's schools.

I've organized the book in an easy-to-use format so you can read the chapters in any order you like, depending on your par-ticular needs. Each chapter focuses on a different aspect of how the K–8 school system works, beginning with its overall structure at the federal, state, district, and local levels and moving through such topics as choosing or changing schools, knowing your rights as a parent, and understanding the relationship between No Child Left Behind, curriculum standards, and high-stakes testing. Each chapter includes background information, tips, ideas, and strate-gies you can use to navigate the school system in the interests of your child, as well as a list of online and print resources to point you to additional information and support.

To make it even easier to dip into the book and pinpoint the specific information that you need, each of the book's twelve chapters is arranged in a series of questions and answers. You can use the book's table of contents or the index to search for topics, questions, and answers to your own specific concerns.

The book's questions came not only from parents but also from teachers, administrators, and students across the United States who shared comments, real-life stories, and strategies for dealing with high-priority issues. You'll find their insights throughout the book. We're all in this together!

In my role as a teacher and as a parent, I too have searched for answers. I know what it's like to help a child start out in a new school, to look for the right school official to work with, and to attempt to navigate a sometimes confusing system. As the mother of a child with dyslexia, I know well the frightening feelings that come with recognizing that something is wrong with your child, but having no idea what to do about it. Despite having taught children at various grade levels, I initially had no idea how to pro-ceed when I saw that my 6-year-old was not reading like the other kids. It was a long, hard struggle to secure for him the education that was rightfully his.

This book is about helping all schoolchildren. By sharing the information I have gained over the years as a parent, teacher, and writer, I hope to provide you with quick, clear answers to your questions. I also hope to stimulate and support your participation in your child's schooling and school system in a way that ensures your daughter or son will get the best education possible.

In the course of writing *Straight Talk About Schools Today*, I have learned a tremendous amount about education, mostly from the many parents and teachers who have been indulgent enough to answer my questions. And in the course of interviewing dozens of moms and dads nationwide, I have heard the same advice again and again: enjoy your child, and be an advocate for your child.

I would love to know how the book's information and ideas have helped you. And if you have tips to share about how you've made inroads into helping your child have a successful school experience, I invite you to pass them along. You can write to me at:

Free Spirit Publishing
217 Fifth Avenue North, Suite 200
Minneapolis, MN 55401-1299
help4kids@freespirit.com

I wish you well!

Judy Molland

HOW PUBLIC EDUCATION WORKS IN THE UNITED STATES

Local school districts and school boards, local superintendents, state superintendents and boards of education, and the federal Department of Education all play a part in our nation's system of education, but how do they all fit together? This chapter will provide a guide to the structure of education in the United States. Delineating clearly the specific responsibilities at each level, it will help you gain an understanding of where to turn when you have a question or problem.

How is the federal government involved in your child's education?

The United States does not have a national school system. In accordance with the U.S. Constitution, the ultimate authority to create and administer education rests with the fifty states, the District of Columbia, and the five territories of American Samoa, Guam, the Mariana Islands, Puerto Rico, and the Virgin Islands.

Most of these entities have delegated authority to operate schools to local governments. But the federal government does provide guidance and funding for educational programs in which both public and private schools take part. The U.S. Department of Education oversees these programs. The mission of the federal Department of Education is to ensure equal access to education for every individual and to promote educational excellence throughout the nation. The idea is to provide assistance to the states, territories, and schools, and to supplement state support, not replace it. In line with this, these are the major activities of the federal Department of Education:

- implementing laws related to federal financial assistance for education

- collecting data and overseeing research on U.S. schools and disseminating this information to educators and the general public

- identifying the major issues and problems in education and focusing national attention on them

- enforcing federal laws prohibiting discrimination in programs and activities that receive federal funds

The Department contributes about 8.3 percent of the total education spending for K–12 schools nationwide.[1] (This can vary widely among individual schools.) Where does this federal money go? The biggest portion goes toward funding the No Child Left Behind Act of 2002 (NCLB), which is a reauthorization of the Elementary and Secondary Education Act (ESEA), brought into law in 1965. NCLB is intended to raise achievement for all students through a series of accountability measures. (See Chapter 8 for more information about NCLB.) Within NCLB, Title I—the program established to help schools with economically disadvantaged students—is the largest recipient of federal funds under President George W. Bush's proposed education budget for 2007. Under this budget of $56.6 billion, approximately 23 percent of the U.S. Department of Education's K–12 funds go to Title I, providing $12.7 billion to local districts. The second largest amount of money in the budget funds the Individuals with Disabilities Education Act (IDEA), providing over $10.7 billion to states and local schools to assist them in educating children with disabilities.[2]

What is the role of state government in your child's education?

Education is by far the largest budget item for the state, territorial, and commonwealth governments within the U.S. Your state or territory makes most of the decisions regarding education policy and administration for your child's school. State governments have the authority to regulate public preschool, elementary, and secondary education; to license private preschool, elementary, and secondary schools; and to license or otherwise regulate homeschooling. In general, private schools are owned and operated by entities that are independent of any government, but each state or territory has its own legal requirements that apply to private schools. The U.S. Department of Education additionally runs a few educational programs in which both public and private schools participate, but these are the exception.

Of the nation's 54.9 million students enrolled in grades preK–12, 48.5 million (88 percent) attend public schools, while private schools educate 6.4 million (12 percent).[3] In addition, another 1.1 million youngsters are homeschooled, making a total of 56 million preK–12 children who receive some form of education.[4]

Generally, policymaking is framed at the state level and is fine-tuned at the local level. Each state and territory has its own laws regulating education. Some laws are similar while others are not. For example, all states require young people to attend school; the age limits vary, however. The compulsory age for starting school may be 5, 6, 7, or 8. Most states require attendance up to age 16, some up to 18. In theory, every child in the U.S. receives at least eleven years of education.[5]

In most states, education policy is developed jointly by the state board of education and the state legislature. State boards of education are bodies of prominent citizens appointed by the legislature or governor or elected by the public. Their job is to set education policy in such areas as standards, instructional materials, and guidelines for textbook adoptions. In addition, in most states the board appoints the state superintendent, the highest education official in state government. Board members generally receive no remuneration for their services. State departments of education, staffed by paid employees of the state, are responsible for implementing the policies set by the board and overseeing the state's school districts, under the direction of the state superintendent.

In general, state legislatures and boards are responsible for:

- chartering or licensing educational institutions to operate within their jurisdictions
- establishing curriculum guidelines
- setting the minimum number of school days
- establishing school health and safety laws
- licensing or certifying school teachers and administrators
- developing policies and regulations governing public elementary and secondary education
- designating and appointing agencies and boards to oversee public education at all levels
- providing funding and technical assistance to local government agencies and schools

If You Want to Influence State-Level Decisions

- Keep abreast of what's happening in your state legislature and with your state board of education. Use resources such as the newspaper, TV, online services, and your school or district's newsletters and reports.

- Connect with other parents at your child's school to discuss the issues and explore ideas for taking action where change is needed. There is strength and power in numbers.

- Join the parent-teacher organization at your child's school so you can get training in how to advocate before government agencies for better programs and higher achievement.

- Become informed on your state's financial situation. Listen to the arguments on all sides of the school finance question and develop informed opinions. Write to your elected officials and tell them about your experience with school budget issues.

- Look for partnerships with other organizations working on similar issues. Learn from and teach others, divide the workload, and reap the benefits of pooled resources.

Parent Power!

In New York, parent advocacy groups have successfully lobbied in cities across the state to increase taxes on the wealthiest residents in order to prevent cuts to city schools. In 2003, as a result of massive lobbying, the state legislature restored 90 percent of the education cuts proposed by the governor that year. One of the biggest events occurred on May 3, 2003, when ACORN (the Association of Community Organizations for Reform Now), the nation's largest community organization of low- and moderate-income families, held a rally for public education at the capitol in Albany; 50,000 people attended the event. Actress and public school parent Cynthia Nixon spoke, as did students who described having to bring textbooks home on alternate nights and walk an hour to school because there were not enough buses. The rally was pivotal in compelling lawmakers to restore funding for education.

How does education work at the local level?

Even though constitutional authority over education is ultimately vested in your state or territorial government, most states delegate day-to-day operation and many aspects of policymaking to local school districts. In other words, it is at this level that much of the nitty-gritty decisions about your child's schooling are made, such as what she's* allowed to wear to school and which textbooks she is required to read.

Each of the over 14,000 school districts in the U.S. oversees the public elementary and secondary schools within its jurisdiction. These districts vary tremendously in size. About 35 percent of the nation's school districts are very small, with fewer than 600 students. By contrast, a third of all U.S. students attend schools in the largest districts. These comprise only 2 percent of the number of districts, but have enrollments of 25,000 or more.[6]

Straight Talk About Schools Today alternates the use of the pronouns "she" and "he," "him" and "her" when talking about individual children. Unless specific note is made, the information applies to girls and boys alike.

A school board whose members can be elected or appointed by other government officials governs local school districts. It is the role of the school board to set policies and oversee the implementation of those policies. Almost anyone can run for a position on the school board; board members may or may not be paid for their service.

One of the most important jobs of school boards is to hire the superintendent—the person who leads the implementation of district goals and manages the day-to-day operations of the school district. The superintendent works with a staff of school district employees, who in most cases are responsible for the following:

- hiring principals and other district staff
- setting teacher and administrator salaries
- administering teacher inservice training
- coordinating school transportation
- allocating budgets among schools and school programs
- overseeing building construction and maintenance
- entering into partnerships with the community for financial and material resources (for example, when the football team receives funding from a local corporation or when a business underwrites the purchase of computers or equipment for a television studio)
- building public relations with the community

Parental involvement—*your* involvement—in school board governance supports the health of public schools in your community. There are a host of ways parents can participate, from running for office on the board to attending and speaking out at board meetings. Most school board meetings are open to the public. School boards generally have several subcommittees that are ideal for parent involvement. Equally important is helping identify and working to elect qualified candidates, including your fellow parents. Elections for the school board are often hotly contested, so it's important to step forward and support candidates you believe will take your schools in the right direction.

Parents on Board

In Cincinnati, Ohio, parents found that just by asking the board, they got a place at the policy-making table. Parent representatives now serve on most of the Cincinnati school board committees, dealing with issues from the selection of textbooks and establishing the school calendar to training for school-based decision-making councils and overseeing school budget decisions.

———

Hearing about planned budget cuts, a coalition of parent groups in Boston, Massachusetts, restored almost $40 million to the city's education budget in 2003. The lengthy process involved speaking out at state budget hearings and school board and city council meetings and attending numerous events. Funding cuts totaling $120 million were slated for the schools. As a result of parent activism, however, that sum was reduced to $81 million.

It's every bit as important for parents to be at the policy table as at the homework table. School board meetings are generally held once a month, and you can make a difference by speaking up on issues that you care about.

How are schools funded?

The funding of elementary and secondary schools in the U.S. is highly decentralized. In general, along with the federal government's 8.3 percent of total funding, about 45.6 percent and 37.1 percent of funding comes from the state and local governments, respectively. The remainder comes from private sources.[7] Almost all federal money is targeted for supporting specific groups, most notably economically disadvantaged students or those needing special education. If your child is in a private school, he may be the beneficiary of education services provided through a federal title program, or he may receive public funds through a state voucher program. In addition, tax credits may be available on a federal or state basis.

Each state legislature decides how it will pay for its public schools, and funding formulas vary. Local property taxes are the major source of local revenue. While the trend is toward more state funding and control, many states, like Illinois, New Jersey, Ohio, and Texas, depend heavily on local property taxes. Usually a local school board sets the property tax rate, and the public votes on this rate in some places. Citizens may also pay other local taxes designated for schools. The state then contributes an additional amount based on its formula. These dollars may come from a state's income, sales, and business taxes, fees, lotteries, and so on. Budgets received from state sources are often allocated on a formula based on the number of pupils enrolled in a district and the size of the local share of the state tax base.

School Finance: A Glossary of Terms

adequacy School funding approach built on the idea that schools should have enough (adequate) money for students to achieve their state's educational goals. Schools may need additional funds to support low-performing students and those with special needs in order to reach state expectations.

average daily attendance (ADA) Average number of students who attend schools over the course of the year. ADA is determined by the total number of days of student attendance divided by the total number of days in the regular school year. This number is usually lower than *enrollment* (see below) because students move, drop out, or get sick. ADA is frequently used for funding formulas.

bonds, bond measures, bond elections Bonds allow school districts to borrow money for large capital investments such as building renovation and new construction. The principal and interest are repaid through increases in local property taxes.

enrollment Count of the students enrolled in each school and district. Since enrollment fluctuates throughout the year as students withdraw and are replaced, states and territories establish a day, usually in September or October, as the date for the official K–12 enrollment count. Enrollment is different from ADA, and since ADA is generally lower than enrollment, ADA is the figure most commonly used for funding purposes.

equity School funding approach built on the idea that states are required to distribute resources fairly to all students no matter where they live. An equity model does not necessarily take into account how much is needed, only that funds are shared equally.

property tax Tax based on a percentage of the value of real estate. May also be assessed against business equipment and inventory.

property wealth Total value of all taxable property in a district divided by the total number of students. This can vary tremendously from one district to the next. For example, imagine two school districts: District A and District B. Both have the same number of students and both plan to assess a 1.5 percent property tax increase. District A, with $500 million in property value, will raise $7.5 million of revenue, while District B, with $100 million in property value, will raise $1.5 million.

Over the past few years, most states have found themselves facing large tax shortfalls and have had to cut their budgets across the board, including in education. With federal, state, and municipal budgets all stressed to the limit, and with equally strapped taxpayers unwilling to override local revenue limits to help schools meet their operating expenses, almost every public school district in the country has been affected with budget reductions.

As local districts are forced to cut budgets, they have become more creative in raising the cash needed for essentials such as new equipment, textbooks, or janitors. Districts often outsource transportation, food service, custodial, and other programs to lower personnel costs. In some districts, children, or more likely their parents, must pay participation fees for extracurricular programs like athletics and fine arts.

As another response to large budget cuts, many school parents and concerned members of the community have turned to setting up foundations. With over 14,000 school districts in the country, and about 5,000 of them now financed partially by foundations, this has become one of the fastest growing movements to raise money for public school education. Public school foundations were born in the 1980s when states such as California and Massachusetts were struggling with school funding. These community-based nonprofit organizations mostly operate independently from the school districts they support. Originally a source of cash for education extras, today they are increasingly being called upon to cover the cost of basic needs such as library books, student assessments, and classroom equipment. All told, education foundations raise about $29 billion annually for public education.

Income from Parent Teacher Association (PTA) or Parent Teacher Organization (PTO) fundraisers frequently buys equipment and supplies that once were considered essential and were purchased with public money. That money is often raised in very original ways:

- In Oregon, parents sold their blood plasma to keep teachers working.

- In Florida, parents promoted the "License for Learning" state automobile license plate to raise funds. When Florida residents buy these plates, the state donates $15 of the license fee to their county's education foundation.

- The Lexington Education Foundation in Massachusetts held an annual trivia contest to raise money for teacher training and school computers.

- At a public school in Manhattan, New York, parents served pizza on Friday nights during winter, followed by a kids' movie in the auditorium. They charged $10 to cover security and the cost of renting the school. Profits helped provide sports equipment and classroom supplies.

- A parents' association at an elementary school in Los Angeles took over the after-school program. Profit from this fully licensed program ($75,000 a year) goes back to the school in the form of a gift to each teacher for classroom supplies.

- An elementary school in Cary, North Carolina, sold custom-designed T-shirts and raised $4,000 to start a character education program, publish school directories, and provide grade-level support funds for the teachers.

Who decides what your child learns?

There is no simple answer to this question. Authority on educational matters is distributed across federal, state, and local boundaries, so that decision makers include elected officials, state bureaucrats, school boards, textbook committees, parents, and individual classroom teachers. What happens in your child's classroom may be influenced by any of these. To further complicate matters, the picture is constantly evolving.

Let's look at the federal level first. There is no standard national curriculum set by law, since the federal government is barred from establishing curriculum. From time to time national commissions announce educational standards and champion educational goals, but these are proposals and are not legally enforceable. The federal NCLB Act mandates a system of accountability requiring public school students in grades 3–12 to take standardized tests to demonstrate their learning. Under NCLB, states must adopt challenging standards to define what children should know at each grade level and then develop high-quality assessments based on those standards.

In practice, what your child is learning at school relative to these standards is determined by your school district, which creates a curriculum framework specifying what students are expected to know by the end of each grade level in language arts, math, science, and social studies. (At this point, social studies testing—although required in some states—is not federally mandated.) This local curriculum framework has to be aligned with the state standards. Thus, both your state and your local school district have a part to play in deciding what your child is learning, especially in those core curricular areas.

In terms of textbook choice, a great deal of variation exists from state to state. Thirteen states specify that the state either determines all instructional materials or publishes a list from which local school districts can choose. In another eight states, state authorities recommend materials, but selection is carried out at the local level. Still other states give over more authority to local districts.

When it comes to controversial issues within content areas—for example, whether and what children are taught about sexuality or evolution, or what literature students are exposed to—either the state board of education or your local school board may be in the position of making decisions.

To learn what the process is in your state, check with the school principal or curriculum coordinator. And if you have a concern about a textbook or other book your child is reading or the way a subject is being taught, your first step should be to speak with your child's teacher. If you are not completely satisfied with the teacher's response, make an appointment with the school principal, who should be open to your concern. If all else fails, take up the issue with your school board, which is required by law to provide time and opportunity for members of the public to speak. And of course, follow the same course of action if you disagree with a decision to *remove* a book or *not* to teach a particular subject.

Who makes the decisions about recess, physical education, and the arts?

The current movement for standards-based improvement began in the late 1980s, and the place of electives during the school day has periodically been squeezed ever since. The enactment of NCLB in 2002 intensified that movement. This, coupled with shrinking funds and increasing demands for technological updating, staff pay raises, and money for facilities, has put enormous pressure on school boards and administrators. As a result, time and money to support recess, physical education (PE), and the arts are generally at a low point.

Recess. According to the national PTA, nearly 40 percent of elementary schools nationwide have either eliminated or are considering eliminating recess. Studies have found that fewer than 25 percent of U.S. children get twenty minutes of physical activity every day.[8] Since most educators agree that children learn better when using mind and body, and that even a fifteen-minute break enhances a child's ability to learn, this is a worrying development. At the same time, concerns about childhood obesity and its effects on children's health are growing. According to the American Obesity Association, approximately 30.3 percent of children ages 6 to 11 are overweight and 15.3 percent are obese.[9]

So who's making the decisions about recess breaks? It is likely to be your child's school, frequently at the determination of her principal. Principals often face difficult choices in this area. Students at an elementary school in Phoenix, for example, used to have morning, lunchtime, and afternoon recess. But when the school's test scores earned it the label "underperforming," the principal made the decision to cut back on recess in favor of instructional time. Children up through fourth grade were allowed morning and lunchtime recess and kids in fifth through eighth grade got a single break at lunch. With the elimination of an afternoon recess and addition of more rigorous instruction, the school earned a "performing" label the following year.

If your child's school is suffering a loss of recess time, and you're concerned about it, start by talking with the principal. You can also work with your PTA or PTO to bring the issue to school-wide attention and discussion.

Physical education. The situation is a bit different for physical education classes because here state boards of education are involved. Although individual districts can make implementation decisions, it is the state that sets the minimum requirements—and these are, indeed, quite minimum. Only two states, Illinois and Massachusetts, have a daily PE requirement for all students in grades K–12, while two additional states, New Jersey and Rhode Island, require it in grades 1–12. Yet, with the exception of Rhode Island, all these states allow students to substitute other activities for their PE credit. Here are some more statistics: Only thirty-six states mandate PE for elementary school students. Of those, just eleven mandate a specific number of minutes per week for elementary schools, and of these only two (Louisiana and New Jersey) meet the national recommendation of 150 minutes a week, or "daily physical education." And only twenty-eight states require elementary PE teachers to be certified to teach PE.[10]

Schools can choose to go beyond the minimum requirements. If you wish to improve the state of physical education at your child's school, consider getting together with some like-minded parents and teachers and lobbying your school board.

The arts. In the case of arts education, your local school board generally makes the budget decisions. A middle school in California saw its final orchestra performance in May 2005, when the local school board decided to cut $8 million from its budget over five years and to eliminate instrumental music instruction in its fifteen schools. A New Hampshire school board elected to eliminate elementary music, art, and physical education programs districtwide.

Still, thanks to concerned and determined parents and school personnel, the outlook is not all gloom and doom. In 2004, an Iowa school board voted to increase the number of art teachers, allowing each elementary school to have its own full-time teacher. Similarly, a school board in Missouri has helped develop an artists-in-the-schools program, working with arts councils to bring artists to the classroom. These examples reinforce a critical point: Don't underestimate the power of your school board—or your power as a parent to influence the choices your board makes.

? Where can you find out more?

American Library Association (ALA)
50 E. Huron
Chicago, IL 60611
800-545-2433
www.ala.org
The ALA provides a guide, including an action plan and suggested activities, for what to do when a book is challenged. Go to their Web site, click "News," and scroll to "Banned Books."

Beyond the Bake Sale by Jean C. Joachim (New York: St. Martin's Griffin, 2003). A very useful guide to fundraising, written by a parent who has helped raise more than $1 million.

Center for Parent Leadership (CPL)
167 W. Main Street, Suite 310
Lexington, KY 40507
859-233-9849, ext. 226
www.centerforparentleadership.org
Founded on the idea that knowledgeable, engaged parents improve student achievement, this organization offers a wide range of materials, workshops, and strategic advice to parents.

National Association for Sport and Physical Education (NASPE)
American Alliance for Health, Physical Education, Recreation
& Dance
1900 Association Drive
Reston, VA 20191
800-213-7193
www.aahperd.org/naspe
This organization offers excellent advice and resources on how to develop school and community efforts to encourage and promote physical activity.

National Coalition for Parent Involvement in Education (NCPIE)
1400 L Street NW, Suite 300
Washington, DC 20005
202-289-6790
www.ncpie.org
NCPIE promotes the involvement of parents and families in education and fosters relationships between home, school, and the community. The Web site offers many helpful resources for parents including a weekly report of public policy issues in U.S. education.

National Education Association (NEA)
1201 16th Street NW
Washington, DC 20036
202-833-4000
www.nea.org
The NEA offers a multitude of resources on how to influence decisions at the state or local level. Go to the site and click "Parents and Community."

National Parent Teacher Association (PTA)
541 N. Fairbanks Court, Suite 1300
Chicago, IL 60611
800-307-4PTA (4782)
www.pta.org
The PTA provides resources on many issues, including how to get involved in decisions affecting education at all levels. Go to the site and click "Parent Resources."

National School Boards Association (NSBA)
1680 Duke Street
Alexandria, VA 22314
703-838-6722
www.nsba.org
NSBA's Web site contains a wealth of information on school governance, school board policies, and school law.

Parents for Public Schools (PPS)
3252 N. State Street
Jackson, MS 39216
800-880-1222
www.parents4publicschools.com
This organization has an excellent publication, "School Boards: Community Representatives Working on Behalf of All Kids," which covers school board roles, parent roles, ideas on how to influence school boards, and much more.

PTO Today
100 Stonewall Boulevard, Suite 3
Wrentham, MA 02093
800-644-3561
www.ptotoday.com
Through the PTO Today Web site, parents can access a number of PTO publications and connect with other parent leaders through an online message board.

Rescuing Recess
www.rescuingrecess.com
In 2006, the national PTA joined the Cartoon Network to launch Rescuing Recess, a campaign that champions the importance of recess for children and works to help keep and revitalize it in schools across the U.S.

SchoolGrants
P.O. Box 177454
Irving, TX 75017
469-235-7357
www.schoolgrants.org
The SchoolGrants Web site provides a host of information on how to go about setting up an education foundation. Go to the site, click "Links," and scroll to "Foundation Resources."

Chapter Notes

1. U.S. Department of Education, "10 Facts About K–12 Education Funding," June 2005.

2. U.S. Department of Education, "Fiscal Year 2007 Budget Summary," February 6, 2006.

3. U.S. Department of Education, Institute of Education Sciences, National Center for Education Statistics, "Digest of Education Statistics, 2005," 2006, Chapter 1.

4. U.S. Department of Education, Institute of Education Sciences, National Center for Education Statistics, "Digest of Education Statistics, 2005," 2006, Indicator 3.

5. Education Commission of the States, "State Notes: Access to Kindergarten, Age Issues in State Statutes," 2007.

6. U.S. Department of Education, Institute of Education Sciences, National Center for Education Statistics, "Public Elementary and Secondary Students, Staff, Schools, and School Districts: School Year 2003–04," February 2006, table C-15.

7. U.S. Department of Education, "10 Facts About K–12 Education Funding," June 2005.

8. National Parent Teacher Association, "Recess Is at Risk, New Campaign Comes to the Rescue," press release, March 13, 2006.

9. American Obesity Association, AOA Fact Sheets, "Obesity in Youth," 2002.

10. National Association for Sport and Physical Education, "Shape of the Nation," Executive Summary, May 2006, pp. 2–3.

CHOOSING A SCHOOL

Choosing a school is important. Since most children spend over 16,000 hours in school between kindergarten and twelfth grade, your efforts to find the best school for your child represent time well spent. It's also true that you will have more or fewer options, depending on where you live. As you consider schools, some of the elements you will want to check out include class size, student-to-teacher ratio, overall student performance, and convenience. And if you're choosing between a public and a private school, remember there are excellent public schools and excellent private schools. What's important is to find the school that's right for *your* child.

? Can you choose which school your child attends?

Each school within a public school district serves students residing in a specific area. To find out which school serves your home address, check with the local district office. Many district Web sites are set up to allow you to type in your address to find the elementary, middle, and high schools for which your child is zoned. Don't assume that the school just down the road is the one your child will automatically be attending. You may be in for a surprise!

Public schools are required to accept the children who reside in their zoned area. But what if you'd prefer that your child go elsewhere? Can your child attend a public school that is not in his neighborhood, one that he is not zoned for? The answer to this question varies among school districts.

For many parents, the word *choice* brings to mind the idea of educational vouchers or transfer options. In fact, there are several choices available in most communities. Find out if your district offers any of these options:

Open enrollment. This program allows you to choose where your child gets an education rather than simply being assigned to a school on the basis of where you live. This means you can choose among schools within your district (intradistrict) or even among districts (interdistrict).

Alternative schools. Designed to provide nurturing environments for students at risk of school failure, these schools enroll some 613,000 students.[1]

Magnet schools. These special-focus schools are also part of the public school system, but may well be located outside of your zoned school boundaries. They usually have something special to offer that is distinct from a regular school, making them an attractive choice to many students, and thereby increasing the diversity of the student population.

Charter schools. These are publicly funded elementary, middle, or high schools that have been exempted from certain rules and regulations that apply to other public schools, in exchange for some type of accountability for producing specific results set forth in each school's charter.

Vouchers. An education or school voucher is a certificate that allows parents to use public funds to pay for their children's education at a school of their choice—usually a private school. Under this system, students attend private schools with the cost of their tuition, or at least part of it, provided by public funds. Five states (Arizona, Florida, Ohio, Utah, and Wisconsin) and Washington, D.C., currently have voucher programs.

Many districts offer all of these options; others may offer only some. Again, to learn what's available in your district, call your district office or check its Web site. Then, with the list of choices in hand, talk to other local parents to learn more about the choices from their perspective. For example, ask what the procedure is to apply for any magnet school. Or you might want to find out how large the local charter schools are, what their focuses are, and if there is a long waiting list.

Students taking advantage of these alternatives to attending the neighborhood school currently make up about 14 percent of overall elementary, middle, and high school enrollment, mainly in large metropolitan areas that offer intradistrict options. In addition, around 300,000 students across the country now attend schools outside their district. Of these, many are special education students traveling to where more appropriate services are offered.[2]

Another aspect of school choice relates to No Child Left Behind (NCLB). Under NCLB, schools are expected to meet certain overall performance standards for students. If your school is a Title I school—a school that receives special federal funding for economically disadvantaged students—and if it has not met performance goals for two consecutive years, NCLB gives you the right to transfer your child to another school in the same district. Federal funds are provided to cover the costs of such a transfer. As long as your child's original school remains in need of improvement, the school district is required to provide transportation for your child to the new school. If student achievement improves at the original school and it is no longer in need of improvement, you can still keep your child at the new school. However, the district does not have to continue providing transportation.

A cautionary note here: Just because a school is designated in need of improvement does not mean that the school is not good for your child. Before rushing off to make a switch, find out why the school received the label. You have the right to move your child to a new school, but there is no law stating that you must exercise this right.

Other choices you may want to consider include sending your son or daughter to a private school or homeschooling your child. You'll find more background on magnet, charter, and private schools later in this chapter. For information about homeschooling, see page 39.

? What makes a good school?

There are several ways to evaluate the quality of a school. Legislation under NCLB requires an annual school report card for each public school. This report card describes characteristics including enrollment size, test scores, ratio of teachers to students, and much more. You should be able to find this information for your local school online or by contacting the district office.

While strong test scores are a reflection that a school is doing its job, statistics alone cannot tell the whole story. There are many other factors to use in evaluating a school—less measurable qualities like a supportive environment or a sense of community. To check out a school's overall environment and quality, nothing can take the place of a personal visit where you can form your own opinion. Here are some important indicators to keep in mind as you visit, and some questions to ask other parents:

The principal is key. The principal sets the tone for a school, so look for someone who supports the teachers and is able to articulate a clear vision of goals for student achievement at every grade level. Be sure to see how the principal interacts with the students. My current principal hangs out with the students at lunch in the cafeteria, plays sports with them, and makes a point of knowing them by name. A principal also needs to be open to the parent community, be able to advocate for the school at the district level, and be a positive force for it in the community at large.

Children should feel that they belong. Check out the mood and atmosphere of the school. Is the building inviting to students and visitors? Does student artwork hang on the walls? Do you see and hear the students being respectful toward each other? Are the teachers friendly and committed to the students and the school? If you happen to be present right after dismissal time, do you see a busy and engaged staff, or are the teachers already heading out of the building? Children find belonging in an environment where their teachers find it as well.

Excellent teaching is vital. As you walk through the school, what do you see in the classrooms? Are all the students involved, or are there pockets of children who appear bored? Is the classroom atmosphere lively? Do the teachers seem enthusiastic about the subject matter? Chances are that if the teachers are excited about what they are teaching, students will feel excited, too. And in addition to a school's test scores, be sure to check out other ways the school measures student achievement, such as through student work and projects.

Every school should have high expectations for all its students. Look to see if the school offers accelerated classes, gifted student programming, and services for students with special needs. And look for signs of enrichment outside the classrooms: field trips to local sources of learning, student plays, instrumental and vocal music activities, athletic programs and contests, and environmental education.

A safe, healthy environment is essential. You need reassurance that your child is disciplined and safe both inside and outside the classroom, so be sure to get details about how the school ensures the physical safety of its students in the classroom, cafeteria, and restrooms, at recess, and when they arrive at and depart from school.

In addition to safety, check out the food and the cleanliness at the school. A nutritious lunch program is well balanced and doesn't rely on canned or processed foods or large amounts of sugar. Take a look at the bathrooms and the gym facilities. Are there doors on the lavatory stalls? Are the walls free of graffiti? Are these areas kept sanitary?

After-school activities are important. Check to see if the school offers sports, clubs, or other extracurricular programs. The sense of community also extends to evening and weekend events that attract students and their families and help create a supportive atmosphere. Some wonderful examples I've encountered in my years teaching are seasonal festivals (including a delightful Maypole celebration) and evening programs that allow classes to present the results of their in-depth studies (such as a "Welcome to Egypt" evening presented by an excited and talented group of fifth graders).

Watch for lots of parent participation. If you see evidence that parents are volunteering in the school, present on campus, and helping in meaningful ways, that's a very strong indicator of a healthy school. Look for an active Parent Teacher Association (PTA), Parent Teacher Organization (PTO), or equivalent organization.

The presence of strong connections across grade levels is a positive indicator. Is the elementary school principal knowledgeable and proud about students' futures, indicating a clear vision for each student from kindergarten through high school? If the middle school offers courses (for example, foreign language) that continue into high school, is there evidence of clear articulation between the middle and high school in regards to curriculum and expectations?

Are there enough books and computer terminals? And how many students are using them? An abundance of computers means nothing if they aren't turned on. Do students choose to visit the media center in their free time? Find out what kinds of library resources are available to students, too.

A very important proviso here is not to take any one factor in isolation. The son of one of my colleagues attended a crowded middle school, housed in a building that was old and in need of renovation and repairs. Yet the teachers were excellent for the most part, and the kids were excited about going to school every day. They were learning well even though the physical condition of the building was less than ideal.

At the end of the day, the most important way to evaluate a school may be how you feel about it. This is not very scientific, but no matter what the local paper says, or what trend the test scores show, if you feel comfortable about a school, you will probably feel comfortable sending your child there. And if you don't, you should keep looking.

What is a magnet school?

Many American students attend public schools called magnet schools, so-named because they "attract" students from all areas of a city or community. Students can choose to attend a magnet school instead of the school closest to their home if they meet the school's selection criteria.

Magnet schools—also known in some areas as focus schools—offer programs designed for students with special abilities, interests, or needs. For example:

- An 11-year-old girl is passionate about computers. She attends a science/technology magnet school.
- A 13-year-old boy has a passion for music and drama. He is enrolled in an arts academy.
- A 10-year-old student who cannot hear attends a magnet school for the deaf and hearing impaired.

Magnet schools were originally established as a tool to further academic desegregation, and while integration remains a theoretical goal of these schools, they sometimes can actually segregate students: some magnet schools attract only students who do well on tests; others may have a distinctive program that interests a particular group, such as Spanish speakers; and sometimes transportation issues may rule out the possibility of children from low-income families attending a magnet school. Many magnet schools have evolved into the "jewels" of their school district, with a reputation for high-quality instruction. Some have taken on a more competitive aspect and are now forced to turn away 80 to 90 percent of the students who apply.

According to the United States Department of Education, more than half of the large urban school districts have magnet school programs as compared to only 10 percent of suburban districts, and very few rural districts.[3]

Is a magnet school right for your child? Here are some questions to consider:

- Are you or your child interested in a different curriculum or instructional approach than what she would receive at her nearest public school?
- Do you feel that your child has needs that would be better served by a magnet school than by her zoned neighborhood school?

▨ How do you feel about sending your child to a school outside of your normal school zone? How well do you think she will adjust?

▨ Are you seeking a school with more racial and ethnic diversity for your child?

▨ Do you want to place your child in a school with greater rigor than her assigned school?

Your child may gain admission to a magnet school using one of a variety of avenues: through first-come, first-served applications; by meeting admissions criteria for the particular school's focus; via lotteries; or as part of the percentage of the school's "set-asides" (reserved enrollment spaces) for neighborhood residents.

Magnet schools don't come one-size-fits-all. Be sure to check out each one individually to determine if it is right for your child and your family.

Magnets Attract . . .

In California. A Northridge, California, mother of a 12-year-old daughter and a 9-year-old son, is a typical example. "Magnet schools have provided wonderful experiences for my children," she says, adding that she feels fortunate to live in the Los Angeles Unified School District, which has more than 160 magnet programs. "As a kindergartner, my daughter was very interested in math and science. I looked at all the magnets and particularly loved Haskell's Math/Science Magnet because it had all kinds of fascinating hands-on activities. I was lucky because my daughter got in and loved it there." With her son in a gifted magnet program at Vena Avenue Elementary School in Pacoima, California, this mom says that she couldn't be happier with the excellent programs and many fine teachers.

In Missouri. The Foreign Language Academy is a magnet school where children in kindergarten through eighth grade experience language immersion. Like all the magnet schools in Kansas City, the Academy draws students from across the city. A parent who spends twenty minutes every day driving her children to the school says, "The Spanish and French language immersion programs and the sense of community we get at the school more than compensate" for the time and logistical challenges of getting there.

In Texas. Magnet students in Houston who live more than two miles away from their campus are eligible for round-trip transportation between district-designated centralized bus stops and their assigned campuses.

To find out about magnet schools in your area, check out your school district's Web site. And if you come up empty, you can always take your idea for a magnet school to the local school board. That's where the decision to start a magnet school is made.

What are charter schools? How do they work?

Charter schools are publicly funded schools that operate apart from many of the regulations that apply to traditional public schools. They have a different organizational model, or charter, which releases them from the regular school administration. Charter schools offer teachers and students more authority to make their own decisions about how and what they learn, for example, but in exchange they are accountable for academic results and for upholding their charter. The charter establishing each school is a performance contract detailing the school's mission, program, goals, students served, methods of assessment, and ways to measure success. Usually a local or state school board grants the charter. The charter's length varies, but the average is three to five years. At the end of the term, the entity granting the charter may or may not renew the school's contract.

According to the fourth-year report of the *National Study of Charter Schools*, the three reasons most often cited to create a charter school are to realize an educational vision, to gain autonomy from bureaucratic restrictions, and to serve a special population.[4] Whatever the reason, the people who start a charter school are usually dissatisfied with the current schooling choices for their children.

Many charter schools are initiated by a visionary parent, teacher, administrator, or community leader. However, starting a charter school is a lengthy process, and no one can do it alone. The first stage is connecting with other like-minded people in the community in order to build a strong founders' group. This group needs to have expertise in a number of areas including curriculum and instruction, financing, education law, fundraising, and assessment of student achievement so it can devise a sound school plan. This plan will eventually evolve into a charter petition, a complicated document which has to be approved by the charter-granting agency (generally a local board of education or county office of education). As you might imagine, this can be a costly business, and it often involves receiving funding from foundations, private donors, and corporate sponsors. Some states also offer grants to help pay for the charter development process.

If you are thinking of selecting a charter school for your child, you are probably interested in high academic standards, small class and school size, innovative approaches, or an educational philosophy in line with your own.

Charters in Charge

Fulton Science Academy in Alpharetta, Georgia, is a good example of what charter schools can offer: it has a highly tailored math and science curriculum that stresses problem solving and working in small groups. Both parents and teachers are dedicated to making the students successful. It is truly a community effort, so much so that there is usually a lengthy waiting list for each grade level.

Natomas Charter School is located in the Sacramento, California, area. Ting L. Sun, Ph.D., is one of its founders. She and Charlie Leo, another middle school teacher in the same district, teamed up to create the school in 1993. Opening with eighty eighth graders, it has now grown to more than a thousand students in four programs. Natomas teachers, students, and families take pride in the school's commitment to its core values: community service, a thematic approach to curriculum, parental involvement, technology, and alternative assessments.

Charter policies and procedures vary from one community to another; some school districts have plenty of experience approving charter schools, while others have never even seen an application. Depending on your state's charter law, such an application may need to be made to the school district, the state board of education, a community college, or even a state university. Generally, the regulating authority welcomes the energy and initiative of people working to set up a charter school, but there is no guarantee that the charter will be granted, however well-developed the application.

Since charter schools are public schools, there is no restriction on who can apply for admission. In fact, the schools are required to conduct outreach and recruitment in all segments of the community they serve. Some schools are very popular. When more students apply than can be accommodated, these schools employ a lottery to randomly determine who will be accepted.

Like all other public schools, charters are not allowed to charge tuition, and they are funded according to enrollment. However, there may be some extra costs involved in sending your child to a charter school: transportation, uniforms, or supplies. In most cases, you are responsible for getting your child to and from school. Still, before deciding a school won't work because of transportation challenges, check with the principal. There may be other parents in your situation, and with the emphasis on parent involvement, many schools have programs in place to help arrange for carpools or public transportation.

Parents who send their child to a charter school often do so out of a clear desire to be actively involved. "All the hands-on stuff is what really connects it for the kids," says a parent of three children at a charter school in Meadowlands, Minnesota. "What connects it for the parents is that they can be directly involved and they don't have layers of bureaucracy to go through when they want to have input in how things are done." Some charter schools may even ask you to sign a contract affirming your involvement with your child's schooling. At the very least, you can expect an intensified set of expectations as to your role in your child's education.

What is a private school?

Beyond the varying choices in public schooling, parents also have the option of enrolling their children in private school. Around 6 million students attend private elementary and secondary schools in this country, or about 12 percent of the total elementary and secondary enrollment. While the term *private school* may make you think of a rich, exclusive establishment far beyond the reach of most of us, in reality there are many different types of private schools. It's also worth noting that while most of these schools charge tuition for their services, a few schools are tuition-free. Likewise, most private schools offer financial aid, which can range from small scholarships to grants and full tuition. Most are coeducational, but single-sex schools are enjoying renewed popularity. There are approximately 400 private boys' and girls' schools in the United States.

Religious schools make up the majority of private schools in the U.S. Sometimes called parochial schools, they are most commonly established and operated by Catholic or Protestant churches. Hebrew and Islamic schools may also be termed parochial. Teachers may be clergy or lay persons, and most are required to be trained educators. In most cases, your child doesn't have to be a member of the related faith to attend the school, but he will usually be required to attend regular religious instruction and prayer in addition to his secular classes. Most religious schools seek accreditation, meaning that they have received the stamp of approval from a regional accrediting authority. Tuition is usually charged, and often the sponsoring religious institution subsidizes the operation of the school.

Independent schools are private, nonprofit schools governed by elected boards of trustees. They are funded through tuition payments, charitable contributions, and endowments, rather than from taxes or religious funds. Any surplus funds that may result from full enrollment, a successful summer program, or gifts are automatically reinvested in the school. Of the 28,000 private schools in the U.S., about 1,500 are independent. Of the latter, nearly two-thirds of these are members of the National Association of Independent Schools (NAIS), which means they have been accredited by a recognized state or regional body and have agreed to practice nondiscriminatory policies. Many accept boarding as well as day students.

Proprietary schools are a third type of private school. These schools, which are relatively new, are run for profit, just like a business. Owners or investors take money out of the schools and may make decisions based on both business and educational considerations. Unlike independent schools, they do not answer to any board of trustees or elected officials, and because of this they can be flexible and respond to requests for change more rapidly. Montessori schools are often proprietary schools. Tuition is comparable to that of private, nonprofit schools.

? What are the main differences between private and public schools?

Here is a breakdown of the differences between private and public schools in several key areas:

Students. Private schools are not required to accept every child, and in many private schools, admission is very competitive. However, although students may be from different neighborhoods, they usually have similar goals and interests. This tends to create a fairly homogenous student body. By contrast, public schools must admit all children in their zoned area, including students with special needs. As a result, the students at public schools generally reflect the neighboring community.

Teachers. Private school teachers may not be obligated by state law to have certification, although this may be required by the school in which they teach. Individual private schools have their own personnel requirements, which often include a college degree and demonstrated working knowledge of the teaching subject area. The laws on hiring and firing teachers may be different in private and public schools. After successfully completing a probationary period, public school teachers are granted tenure by law. The same tenure laws do not apply to private school teachers. Teachers in public schools are required to hold a college degree and a teaching license from the state, or at least be working toward state certification.

Governance. Private schools are not limited by as many state and federal regulations as public schools. Since private schools are funded independently, they are not subject to the limitations of state education budgets and therefore have more latitude in designing what your child learns and how she learns it. Public schools must follow all federal, state, and local laws in educating children, including what and how your child learns. Private schools follow many of the same laws as related to the safety and care of students as public schools.

Class size. Private schools are generally committed to providing small classes and individual attention to students and so tend to have smaller class sizes and lower student-teacher ratios than do many public schools. In 1998, President Bill Clinton proposed a national effort to reduce class size in the first, second, and third grades. Many states have since provided funding to keep public school class sizes small in kindergarten through third grade. So, while in public school your child may enjoy smaller class size in the primary grades, she will probably be in slightly larger classes once she reaches fourth grade.

Curriculum. Private schools can create their own curriculum and assessment systems, although they often use the same, or similar, materials and tests as the local public schools. They also have the potential to create specialized programs for children. For example, private schools may incorporate art or science in all classes, or take students on multi-day trips that blend elements from across the curriculum. By contrast, public schools offer a general program that usually includes math, English, reading, writing, science, social studies, and physical education. Most of the public school curriculum is mandated by the state, which also makes standardized tests obligatory.

While these are generalized differences between private and public schools, every educational institution, private and public, has its own culture. The only way you can find out about that climate and determine if it's the right fit for your child is by visiting a school and experiencing it for yourself.

Do children receive the same special education services in a private school as in a public school?

There are many private schools established specifically to educate young people with special needs. Because of this focus, these schools are often able to succeed where public schools cannot. At the same time, however, private schools are not legally obligated to provide any such services, and many private schools offer either limited or no special education services at all. In such a case, if your child is in a private school and has been diagnosed with a reading difficulty, perhaps he will be pulled out once a day for an extra half-hour of reading instruction. In addition, special education services for the child in a private school may be available through the local public school. But the bottom line is that if a private school does not receive any public funding and is not voluntarily providing special education services for your child, there is little you can do legally to obtain those services.

If your child has special needs, your local public school is required by law to meet those needs. Any student attending a school that receives public funds of any sort is guaranteed a "free appropriate public education" (FAPE). For students with disabilities, this means they may be eligible for services under one of two laws: the Individuals with Disabilities Education Act (IDEA) or Section 504. Under IDEA, your child will receive an Individualized Education Program (IEP)—an education program that provides instruction in a way that is fundamentally different from the way other children are learning. A 504 plan is less sweeping than special education and is used where a child can learn from the regular education curriculum but needs some special accommodations to help him learn. Typical modifications include a seat in the front row of the class or the right to extra time on tests.

Given this law of the land, most public schools do have special education programs or teachers. But while some public school systems have specialized schools to support children with multiple special needs, and do a fantastic job, in other systems, parents may have more of a struggle to get the special education that is their child's right. With limited amounts of funding, special education can receive a low priority in the budget, particularly if the percentage of students needing services is relatively small. One of the goals of NCLB is to ensure that, in fact, *all* students are educated to their highest potential.

Do students in private schools need to pass state benchmark tests and meet graduation requirements set by public schools?

The short answer is no. Private schools can create their own curriculum and assessment systems. Many, however, do choose to use state standardized tests. When private school students take standardized achievement tests, they generally perform better than their public school counterparts. For example, the National Assessment of Educational Progress (NAEP)—the federal test known as "The Nation's Report Card"—details information for the nation and specific geographic regions of the country. In 2000, as in previous years, private school students performed higher than public school students on the NAEP tests. Private school average scores were above those of their public school counterparts on the fourth-grade reading test and on the fourth-, eighth-, and twelfth-grade science and mathematics proficiency tests.[5] (Note: NAEP is only given in these three grades.)

Likewise, graduation requirements for private schools are decided by each school and are not subject to any state requirements. In practice, however, many private schools align themselves with private school associations such as NAIS, which mandate graduation requirements. Thus, if your child is in a private school, she will have to meet graduation requirements at her school, but they may vary from those set by your state. They are likely to be more demanding than those at your local public school, but they will probably not include a mandatory high school exit exam, an exam required of public high school students. (For a broader discussion of state benchmark tests, see Chapter 9.)

Choosing the right school for your child is a weighty responsibility, but you don't have to do it alone. Researching options online is a good place to start; visiting more than one school, talking to faculty and staff, and making contact with school parents are just as important. Finally, make sure your child visits prospective schools, too, and be sure to take her perspective fully into account.

Where can you find out more?

Alliance for School Choice
5080 N. 40th Street, Suite 375
Phoenix, AZ 85018
602-468-0900
www.allianceforschoolchoice.org
The Alliance for School Choice is a leading source of information on school vouchers both in the U.S. and abroad.

California Charter Schools Association
818 W. 7th Street, Suite 910
Los Angeles, CA 90017
213-244-1446
www.myschool.org
If you are interested in opening a charter school, the Web site for this organization offers "How Do I Start a Charter School?"

Center for Education Reform (CER)
1001 Connecticut Avenue NW, Suite 204
Washington, DC 20036
202-822-9000
www.edreform.com
CER provides contact information and profiles of charter schools nationwide.

Council for American Private Education (CAPE)
13017 Wisteria Drive, #457
Germantown, MD 20874
301-916-8460
www.capenet.org
CAPE is a coalition of national organizations and state affiliates serving private elementary and secondary schools. Visit the Web site for information on member organizations and associations for religious and nonreligious private schools and a school locator you can use to find all types of private schools in your area including Catholic, Protestant, Evangelical, Jewish, Islamic, independent, Waldorf, and Montessori.

GreatSchools
301 Howard Street, Suite 1440
San Francisco, CA 94105
415-977-0700
www.greatschools.net
The GreatSchools Web site offers basic information about all primary and secondary schools in the United States, including public, private, and charter schools. Detailed information is available about elementary and high schools in Arizona, California, Texas, and Florida.

Home Education Magazine
P.O. Box 1083
Tonasket, WA 98855
800-236-3278
www.home-ed-magazine.com
Home Education offers plenty of information to get you started if you are interested in learning about homeschooling.

Magnet Schools of America (MSA)
1012 14th Street NW, Suite 903
Washington, DC 20005
202-824-0672
magnet.edu
MSA can provide you with the latest information on magnet schools and programs in the U.S.

National Association of Independent Schools (NAIS)
1620 L Street NW
Washington, DC 20036
202-973-9700
www.nais.org
NAIS provides a searchable database of member schools to assist parents in their research about independent schools in their area.

PSK12.com
www.psk12.com
This Web site provides rankings of public schools in 42 states. For a small fee, PSK12 will provide a detailed analysis of the schools in your area.

SchoolMatch

6167 Deeside Drive
Dublin, OH 43017
614-890-1573
www.schoolmatch.com
SchoolMatch provides information about public and private schools in all 50 states and, for a small fee, offers a detailed school report card that compares the schools in your district with others in the nation.

SchoolMatters

www.schoolmatters.com
This Web site by Standard & Poor's offers a wide array of information on public schools and tools for analyzing reports about your school's performance.

United States Department of Education

400 Maryland Avenue SW
Washington, DC 20202
800-872-5327
www.ed.gov
The U.S. Department of Education provides information at their Web site to help parents find public schools, school districts, charter schools, and private schools. Click "Parents" and then click "Find Schools and After-Care."

Chapter Notes

1. U.S. Department of Education, Institute of Education Sciences, National Center for Education Statistics, "Contexts of Elementary and Secondary Education: Public Alternative Schools for At-Risk Students," 2003.

2. U.S. Department of Education, Institute of Education Sciences, National Center for Education Statistics, "Trends in the Use of School Choice, 1993–1999," 2003.

3. *Public School Review*, "What Is a Magnet School?" 2007.

4. U.S. Department of Education, Office of Research and Improvement, "The State of Charter Schools 2000: Fourth-Year Report," January 2000, pp.16–19.

5. *Public School Review*, "Public School vs. Private School," 2007.

GETTING STARTED
IN KINDERGARTEN

You probably still remember your first day at school, or at least you can recall some images from those early days. Starting kindergarten is a major milestone for your child and for you. For many parents, excitement about this new beginning will be tinged with some regret that their baby is growing up and some fear that they can no longer protect their little one from the outside world. The best way to deal with these concerns is to prepare your child well.

? How do you enroll your little one in kindergarten?

Depending on the state, the initial age for compulsory school attendance varies from 5 to 8.[1] However, while kindergarten attendance is optional in most states, almost all districts are required by law to *offer* a kindergarten program. Find out the regulations regarding the age at which your child can enter kindergarten. In most cases, your child must be at least 5 years old, but it's important to determine the exact date by which he must reach this age—usually between July 31 and December 31, though this varies by state and sometimes by school district.

Pre-registration usually takes place in spring for the following fall, so early spring is a good time to start thinking about where your child will attend school and what his kindergarten class will be like. If your district offers school choice, it's a great idea to visit a few schools and to imagine your child in the various settings. Remember that not every program is perfect for every child. Some children thrive in a program with more direction, some with less.

Half Day or Full?

Another issue to consider is how long your child's school day should be. Across the United States, 60 percent of kindergartners now attend a full-day program.[2] Still, since only nine states require districts to offer full-day kindergarten, your options will depend on where you live. For parents who work during the day, full-day programs often make the most sense, since they limit the number of transitions a child must make, reducing stress for both child and parent.

You will need to fill out registration and emergency medical referral forms when you enroll your child. While specific requirements may vary, you will probably be asked to provide the following:

- Proof of your child's age and identity: a birth certificate or other reliable document such as a passport, hospital birth record, or adoption record.

- Proof of residence: your driver's license, voter registration card, utility bill, rent statement, or any official document showing both your name and address in order to establish residency. As far as immigrant status goes, the Supreme Court ruled in 1982 that states could not deny any child, including undocumented immigrants, access to free public education from kindergarten through high school. In most states, school officials are instructed that they don't have to ask about citizenship.

Records of vaccination and immunization against specific diseases. Check with your school district to find out which they require.

Getting Ready for Your Child to Enter Kindergarten: A Checklist

☑ Choose the kindergarten program your child will attend.

☑ Obtain enrollment information. Do this by checking online, calling the district or school, or stopping at the school office. Read the information and note questions, key dates, and deadlines. Schools are also required to provide information on developmental stages and what to expect in kindergarten along with practical information about scheduling and procedures.

☑ Schedule an appointment with your child's healthcare provider to make sure health records and immunizations are current.

☑ Visit the school by attending an open house or taking a tour.

☑ Arrange to meet the teacher, learn more about what your child will experience in the classroom, and discuss any ideas or concerns about your child.

☑ Learn how you can become involved in the classroom, school activities, and the parent organization.[3]

What other school procedures do you need to know about?

Although there are slight variations around the country, guidelines similar to the following are likely to apply:

Absences. A note from a parent is necessary to excuse any absence and must be submitted within a few days of the child's returning to school. Lawful absences are those due to student illness, death in the immediate family, religious observances, hazardous weather, school or state emergencies, or other activities approved by your local school authority. Family travel is generally not considered an excused absence, except in unusual circumstances. However, if your family needs to make a trip, check with the teacher or principal about getting approval.

Backpacks. Schools generally encourage all children to have backpacks to carry books, notebooks, and other school supplies. Remember to check your child's backpack regularly, since schools often send home notices, newsletters, and other information with their students. And check too that your child's backpack is not causing health problems. It might if she is walking to school and carrying more than 10 to 20 percent of her body weight in her backpack or if she is wearing her backpack on only one shoulder.

Bus transportation. The rules governing bus transportation vary widely from state to state. Many districts provide bus transportation to students who live more than one or two miles from school. Sometimes transportation is available to students who live closer if safety or other factors warrant it. The situation for before- and after-school programs also varies: in some cases, these programs will provide transportation from the school to their site, while in others, parents have to drive or pick up the tab for bus service. Check with your local district to get specific details.

Dress code. Your child will be expected to wear appropriate clothing to school. Children need to wear clothes that allow freedom of movement for playing and activities, and they need appropriate outerwear for wet or cold weather. Clothing that offends others or interferes with the educational process is inappropriate; most schools have specific guidelines about what's acceptable. Some public schools have uniforms, in which case you'll need to find out exactly what is required.

Meals. In general, the school will make lunch available for your child and also may offer breakfast. To avoid having students carrying money every day, many schools have set up a system for parents to deposit money in an account at the cafeteria. Students receive a personal identification number (PIN) that they use to make purchases from the account. In some school districts, money for lunch and milk is just a click away. Parents can access an online account and replenish their children's lunch money via credit card or even set up automatic payments so the milk money never runs dry.

Your child may be eligible for free or reduced-price meals if your household income and family size meet federal guidelines. The United States Department of Agriculture (USDA) publishes income guidelines used in determining eligibility both for free and reduced-price meals and for free milk. Schools that participate in the National School Lunch Program (and Commodity School Program), School Breakfast Program, and Special Milk Program for Children must follow these federal guidelines. Ask at your child's school or go online to the school's Web site for an application form.

School supplies. At the start of every school year, students receive a list of needed school supplies, such as pencils, markers, paper, and binders. Wait until you receive a copy of this list from your child's school before you head out to purchase school supplies. It may also be available on the school's Web site. If you do not get this list before school starts, simply equip your child with a few pencils and some paper for the first day. Some elementary schools call on parents to buy items such as glue sticks, hand sanitizer, and facial tissues to be shared with everyone in the classroom; some even ask for money to purchase these pooled supplies. Contact the school office if you are unable to provide the required supplies.

Student pickup. In theory, only parents or legal guardians and persons they authorize in writing may pick up children from school. You can designate these approved individuals on the emergency card that must be completed at the beginning of the school year. Prior to the pickup time, you may also send your child's school a note authorizing a specific individual to pick up your child. On those occasions, your child's school may contact you by phone, just to make sure the arrangements are correct. The school also may ask the authorized person for photo identification before releasing your child. It's all in the interests of your little one's safety.

Not all schools actually exert this much vigilance, so you may want to check on how safe the arrival and departure procedures are at your child's school.

Is your child ready for kindergarten?

You've gathered all the information about entrance requirements for your local school's kindergarten, but your child's birthday falls right at the cutoff date, and you're still not sure if he is going to be ready. Experts advise that social and emotional readiness are critical for young children's early school success. It's just as important for your child to be able to form good relationships with peers and to follow directions as it is for him to recognize his ABCs and master the use of a crayon or scissors. When your child enters kindergarten, he should have:

- a sense of confidence and enough independence to enjoy doing tasks alone
- a desire to explore and have new experiences outside the home
- the ability to solve simple problems and play cooperatively with peers
- sufficient verbal skills to communicate with adults and children
- the ability to deal with the physical demands of a new environment, such as stairs and the toilet*

How can you know if your child is ready? If your child is already in an early childhood program such as childcare, preschool, or pre-kindergarten, it may be relatively easy to evaluate how he fits these criteria. If your child is not part of one of these programs, or you're still unsure about his readiness, a good way to determine how he will fit into his kindergarten is to visit the school while class is in session and picture him in the classroom. While there, check to find out if there is a list of things he is expected to know prior to entering the school. Once you have a clear sense of where your child may need a little extra help, you can put some time into building that particular skill with him.

Although many school districts are reluctant to accept children early for kindergarten, some will make an exception in the case of gifted children. These children learn rapidly, and for them, early entry into kindergarten may be essential. Most states now make provisions for the identification of gifted children. (For more information, see Chapter 11.)

Having your child wait another year before starting kindergarten is probably appropriate if you, your child's early childhood

---

*Some children have physical, cognitive, or behavioral challenges that qualify them for special services. Determining readiness for kindergarten in these situations involves working closely with school personnel.

program director, or the counselors and administrators at your new elementary school believe that your child is not ready. It is much better to delay now than to have him repeat a year later on.

It's Not Always Easy to Decide

Consider these two stories parents have shared.

Lara. The cutoff date for kindergarten was September 1. Lara was turning 5 on October 9, but her mom decided she was ready for kindergarten. The local school wasn't willing to make an exception, so Lara's mother found a charter school that accepted her daughter based on the behavior Lara exhibited while registering and on her preschool teacher's recommendation. To Mom's delight, Lara excelled. Although she was almost the youngest in the class, she was in the top reading group and began working on sight words before many of her classmates. Kindergarten also helped with her socialization, as she became much more friendly and relaxed with the children in her class. Lara is in third grade now. She and her mom report that she continues to thrive academically and socially and that she loves school.

Miguel. Miguel made the kindergarten cutoff date by one day. At first, everything went well. He was in the advanced reading group, had excellent grades, and was well liked by teachers and kids. But by second grade, things began to slide. Miguel no longer had many friends, and he began to find the schoolwork much harder. The age difference between Miguel and his classmates—one-half to one full year—became much more relevant. Miguel's parents arranged for testing, but there was no evidence of a learning disability. It became clear that although their son was very smart, developmentally he was behind his older classmates.

Now, in the third grade, Miguel's peers are turning 9, while he has just turned 8. His teachers report that he doesn't understand much of what he is reading. Although he is working twice as hard to keep up, he's just getting by. He spends hours on homework assignments, refusing to give up, and somehow manages to maintain a positive attitude. Distressed to see their child struggling so much, and supported by school officials, Miguel's parents have made the decision to move their son back into second grade.

As with so many other parenting questions, there is no easy answer regarding whether to send your child to kindergarten early. You know your child best, so following your instincts is likely to be the best way to proceed. But situations can change. Like Miguel's parents, if you do decide to enroll your daughter or son in kindergarten at a younger age than most, be sure to keep a careful eye on your child's progress.

? How can you best prepare your child for kindergarten?

Read to your child every day in a way that is enjoyable for both of you. Since children learn through play, play with her. Break out simple board games; play with magnetic letters, take a walk through the neighborhood to look for letters on street signs; sing together; create Lego constructions. Limit screen time: television, video games, and playing on the computer are passive activities that are high in stimulation. Your child may find the constant action appealing, but it will decrease her attention span. Children need active playtime to develop mental, physical, and social skills. The time your child sits in front of a video screen is time she's not involved in other activities such as cutting and pasting, reading, learning to get along with other kids, and exploring her world.

Another way to ready your child for kindergarten is to enroll her in a preschool program, if possible. For one thing, this will help you evaluate how she interacts in a classroom setting. If preschool isn't an option for you, try to arrange for your child to spend part of the day away from you now, so that when she goes to kindergarten, she won't have a difficult time separating. For example, many parents arrange to swap childcare with another family once a week for a few hours. This costs nothing, gives you some time to catch up on your own activities, and gives your child the chance to have a good time playing with other kids under the supervision of another adult. Alternatively, arrange to have a relative or close friend spend some time with your child.

Talking to your child about school also will help to relieve stress for both of you. Try reading books about kindergarten to her. Be ready to answer any questions she has about what school will be like. Reassure her if she has fears or anxieties. One way to do this is to give her an idea of what her kindergarten day will look like. Or you can plan for your child to visit her new school.

Practice Runs

One parent thought it would be helpful to practice the morning routine of going to school. A few days before school began, he took his child through the steps of waking up, eating breakfast, and walking to school with an older neighbor child. This helped create a morning schedule, and it helped the child become familiar with her new morning pattern. As a side benefit, the parent also felt better about sending his daughter off to kindergarten, knowing that he had done all he could to facilitate her transition to "big kid" school.

If you are feeling anxious about letting go of your baby, do your best not to transmit those concerns to your child. Picking up on parental discomfort can leave children feeling less confident as they take this new step in their lives.

Finally, don't forget to go over some practical skills with your child: getting dressed, buttoning clothes, fastening shoes, and snapping snaps. Make sure your child knows your address and phone number so that you can be reached if she needs you.

Should you delay kindergarten entrance in order to boost your child's academic performance?

Academic redshirting is the name given to the practice that involves parents keeping their child out of kindergarten for an extra year even though the child's birthday meets the relevant cutoff date. The idea of redshirting dates back to the late 1980s, when some schools felt pressured by mandatory testing to make the early elementary grades more academically rigorous. Today's even greater emphasis on meeting standards has increased academic demands on the lower elementary grades, reaching all the way to kindergarten. Some parents decide to hold their children out of kindergarten until they are a year older because they feel their youngsters will not be able to cope with the high academic demands. Other parents decide to postpone their child's entry into school in order to provide what they believe to be an academic edge—an extra year to gain knowledge, skills, and maturity.

When parents redshirt their kindergarteners, the age gap within one class can often be 18 months or more. This poses a challenge for teachers, who are concerned that while younger children may struggle, older children may get bored and act out.

Starting school at a later age doesn't necessarily translate into an academic edge. Deborah Stipek, Dean of the School of Education at Stanford University, found in a report conducted by the National Institute for Early Education Research (NIEER) that, on average, older children did not academically outperform their younger peers.[4] Nor, as Stipek's own research has found, are there necessarily any social or emotional benefits to being older in the grade.[5]

Each school district has a slightly different approach regarding the best time to start kindergarten. If you are concerned, begin by contacting your district office to find out what they suggest. If you disagree, try talking to other parents of kindergartners and find out their experience. The bottom line is that if you believe your child is ready for kindergarten, then you should enroll him in his age-appropriate class. If not, you will likely want to have him wait.

Will kindergarten for your child be very different from when you were in school?

Much has been made of the "push-down" of academic curriculum into the kindergarten year. Many skills that were once taught in first grade are now being introduced in kindergarten. You will still find the small chairs and finger-painting, but in general, there is more formal learning going on in kindergarten classrooms than a generation ago.

The shift from a play-based curriculum to a greater emphasis on academics is not simply the result of the pressure to prepare students to meet rising standards and to pass standardized tests once they get to third grade, but also is due to the emerging understanding regarding brain development. New research is indicating that the brain develops rapidly in the early years of life and that young children may be capable of much more than was previously thought.[6] In response to both research and more defined academic standards, kindergarten classrooms are now filled with plenty of toys and learning materials that offer interesting and challenging activities.

In many ways, clearly established, high expectations that all children are intended to meet are a good thing. As a teacher in Lincoln, Nebraska, puts it, "What's happening is that as our nation moves toward a greater articulation of standards and their assessment, the questions about what children need to know and do at each grade level, including kindergarten, are becoming much more clearly stated." At the same time, child-development experts stress the importance of a developmentally appropriate curriculum for kindergartners. This means that your child should be learning those academic skills within a play-based curriculum— one that takes into account the wide range of skill levels present in the classroom, and that allows each student to reach maximum potential. Your child also should be learning social skills such as cooperation, negotiation, and working well within a group.

In recent years, there has been much talk about the importance of play. The American Association for the Child's Right to Play was specifically created to protect and preserve play as a fundamental right of children. The association explains that play makes possible maximum self-development by facilitating creativity, individuality, and social, physical, and intellectual growth.

What Will Your Child Learn in Kindergarten?

Here's a sampling of what your child might be expected to know by the end of kindergarten:

Reading. Students know about letters, words, and sounds. They apply this knowledge to read simple sentences.

Writing. Students write words and brief sentences that are legible.

Listening and speaking. Students listen and respond to oral communication. They speak in coherent sentences.

Number sense. Students use estimation strategies in computation and problem solving that involve numbers using the ones and tens places.

Measurement and geometry. Students identify common objects in their environment and describe the geometric features.

What should you expect to see in a developmentally appropriate kindergarten class?

If you ask any number of educators and parents this question, you will probably get an equal number of different answers. Not every program is perfect for every child. Still, there are certain basics that most educators emphasize. Look for:

- ☑ **Children learning by using their hands and senses,** by experimenting and exploring, and by finding out for themselves. The classroom and school environment are their laboratory, and teachers are both guides and assistants in their learning process.

- ☑ **A combination of formal (teacher-initiated) and informal (child-initiated) activities.** Investigations and projects allow children to work both on their own and in small groups.

- ☑ **A preponderance of activities that feature play-based, hands-on learning** in small groups. As the year progresses, large-group activities become a bit longer in preparation for first grade.

- ☑ **A reasonable class size,** which means no more than twenty-five children with two adults, or fifteen to eighteen children with one adult.

- ☑ **Teachers who design the curriculum flexibly** so that each child learns what she is ready for and moves at her own optimal pace.

- ☑ **Children's work displayed in the classroom** (and school) in a way that clearly shows the work is valued.

- ☑ **Teachers who engage the children in conversation** both individually and as a whole group. Children are encouraged to describe what they're doing and to communicate their ideas.

- ☑ **Teachers who value parents' input** and have frequent dialogue with them about what's going on in the classroom and about their child's progress.

What about pre-kindergarten?
If your district offers pre-kindergarten,
is that something you should consider?

The answer is a resounding "Yes!" say researchers at the National Institute for Early Education Research (NIEER). In a report published in December 2005, they concluded that children who attend high-quality state preschool programs with well-trained teachers make significant academic gains, regardless of their families' economic status.[7] Your ability to take advantage of this information will depend on what's available in your community, because the picture varies dramatically across the U.S. Forty-three states currently fund early learning programs for young children before formal schooling traditionally begins, but these programs' implementation can take different forms. For example, you may be taking your 4-year-old to a school, while your neighbor has her child enrolled at a community center, and another neighbor takes his child to a Head Start program. Whatever the program, be sure to check it out personally to make sure it meets your needs and the needs of your child.

One final note: Be sure to give your child a chance to talk about his school day. Let him know it's okay to have mixed or even unhappy feelings. Let him know that you, too, have both good and bad days. Helping your child overcome his doubts about kindergarten will help him feel good about himself and confident in facing other new situations.

Where can you
find out more?

Pages 18–20 will point you to a number of organizations, including the National Education Association and the Parent Teacher Association, to help you understand the U.S. education system and become an active presence in your child's schooling. Here are other organizations and resources that can be of help as you enroll your child in school for the first time.

The Mommy and Daddy Guide to Kindergarten by Susan Bernard with Cary O. Yager (Chicago: Contemporary Books, 2000) is a helpful and information-packed guide for parents whose children are taking the exciting—yet scary—first step into kindergarten.

Expert advice from educators, doctors, psychologists, and parents is offered in an easily accessible A-to-Z format.

**National Association for the Education
of Young Children (NAEYC)**
1313 L Street NW, Suite 500
Washington, DC 20005
800-424-2460
www.naeyc.org
NAEYC is the nation's largest organization of early childhood professionals dedicated to the quality of children's early education. To receive the free brochure "A Good Kindergarten for Your Child," send a self-addressed, stamped envelope along with your request.

National Center for Early Development and Learning (NCEDL)
University of North Carolina at Chapel Hill
Campus Box 8185
Chapel Hill, NC 27599
919-966-0867
www.ncedl.org
NCEDL offers the latest in news and research about the cognitive, social, and emotional development of children from birth to age 8. The Web site contains research articles and reports and a substantive list of outside resources.

National Institute for Early Education Research (NIEER)
120 Albany Street, Suite 500
New Brunswick, NJ 08901
732-932-4350
http://nieer.org
NIEER supports early childhood educational initiatives by providing objective information based on research. The organization can answer your questions about what's going on in early childhood education today.

"The 100 Greatest Children's Books of All Time" is one of several articles available at the Parenthood Web site (www.parenthood. com). Type "articles" in the search box and scroll down for articles on award-winning books, both modern and classic, including NAPPA's (National Parenting and Publications Awards) annual lists of recommended books for preschoolers and kindergartners.

The Read-Aloud Handbook by Jim Trelease (New York: Penguin, 2006) is so popular that it is now in its sixth edition. The book answers all the "why," "how," and "what" questions about effective reading aloud. It is also a terrific resource for books to read to your child.

Scholastic
557 Broadway
New York, NY 10012
212-343-6100
www.scholastic.com
Scholastic offers a multitude of resources for and about the early learner, including *Your Early Learner: Parent & Child*, a bimonthly magazine designed especially for parents with young children attending childcare, preschool, and kindergarten programs.

Your Child's Growing Mind by Jane M. Healy (New York: Broadway Books, 2004) has been a cornerstone for parents and educators since it was first published in 1987. Now revised and updated to reflect recent findings in brain research, the book guides parents, teachers, and caregivers as they gauge the level of development of an individual child's brain.

Chapter Notes

1. Education Commission of the States, *StateNotes,* "Access to Kindergarten: Age Issues in State Statutes," February 2005.

2. Education Commission of the States, "Kindergarten: Quick Facts," 2007.

3. National Education Association, "A Parent's Guide to a Successful Kindergarten Transition," May 2005.

4. National Institute for Early Education Research, "Frequently Asked Questions: Is there a research base that can be used to inform decisions about state kindergarten cutoff dates?" 2007.

5. Society for Research in Child Development, Social Policy Report: "At What Age Should Children Enter Kindergarten?" vol. XVI, no. 2, 2002.

6. National Academies Press, Institute of Medicine, "From Neurons to Neighborhoods: The Science of Early Childhood Development," 2000.

7. National Institute for Early Education Research, "The Effects of State Pre-Kindergarten Programs on Young Children's School Readiness in Five States," December 2005, p. 15.

CHANGING SCHOOLS

With statistics telling us that about 50 percent of the population moves every five years, plenty of parents will face moving their child to a new school at some point in her educational journey. Leaving behind treasured friends and familiar places and activities is stressful for parent and child alike. You'll want to do all you can to ease the anxiety associated with a school transition. The same is true if, moving or not, you've decided to change schools, and your child is facing life in a totally new environment. How can you best help your child deal with new surroundings and all the anxieties about starting over? While Chapter 2 provides information on selecting a good school when starting out, this chapter looks at the issues associated with switching schools midstream.

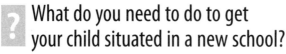

What do you need to do to get your child situated in a new school?

Your first step is to find the right school, so collect information about the schools in your new neighborhood. There are a few ways to go about doing this. GreatSchools is a Web site that offers information about all elementary and secondary public, private, and charter schools in the United States (www.greatschools.net). The United States Department of Education's Web site also maintains similar information (www.ed.gov). If you're interested in a private school, you can check online with the National Association of Independent Schools (www.nais.org) or the Council for American Private Education (www.capenet.org). Closer to your new home, try the local Chamber of Commerce, the Welcome Wagon organization, and local realtors and rental agencies. If you are moving to a new job, you can always ask the advice of your new employer.

If you can, involve your child in making this decision. The unknown is scary for all of us, so take your child with you to look at potential neighborhoods and schools. Although this may seem time-consuming and expensive, it's a great way to help your child make the adjustment to his new environment. With a younger child this may be unrealistic; in that case, take a camera with you when you go. Your child will appreciate the pictures, and it will help him make the transition.

If you're relocating to a new community or neighborhood, it's probably going to be a stressful time for you, too. Amidst all you need to do, set aside time to focus entirely on your child and his concerns. Visit both the district office and the school to pick up as much information as you can, including summer reading lists, student and parent handbooks, and a school district calendar.

Arrange to have your child's records sent to the new school in advance. If you have moved from one state to another, check with the school or with a healthcare provider to see if your child meets the new state's regulations about immunizations.

You can request placement testing in all subjects that the school teaches at different ability levels. This is important because what is taught at a given grade level can vary significantly from one community or state to another. You don't want your child to find himself struggling in math, for example, because at the new school he's expected to know material that he has not been taught.

If your child has a learning difference, physical challenge, or other special need, your early research will include looking at the special services available in the new school. Recognize that there will be differences in services from school to school and district to district. Expect that your son or daughter will need some time to adjust. Tell your child all about the special education program.

Talk to the principal, resource teachers, and other parents involved in special education about any concerns such as wheelchair accessibility, classroom accommodations, or pull-out programs. (See Chapter 11 for more information about special education and gifted programming.)

Try to meet your child's new teacher either before the school year begins or before your child's first day if this is a midyear switch. If your child is in middle school, contact the school office to arrange to meet his counselor and his homeroom or advisory teacher.

At most schools, the teacher or counselor can arrange for a new student to have another child show him around for a day. Ask your child's teacher to consider doing this and to make sure that your child has a buddy when students are working in pairs or groups. Keep in mind that academics may not be your child's first concern, and initially they most likely shouldn't be yours either. Your child probably won't be able to concentrate on studying until he feels comfortable in his new surroundings. For middle schoolers the move can be especially stressful. Encourage your child to make a connection with one or two people to start out. You can also talk to the school counselor and ask for friendship buddies or peer helpers to smooth the way.

How can you ease the transition?

While entering a new school may seem daunting for your child, it also can be a very exciting time, depending on the circumstances of the move. Approach the transfer in a positive manner, pointing out all the advantages to be gained: new friends, the adventure of starting fresh at a different school, and a variety of activities and extracurricular opportunities to explore. Your child will take her cue from you, so it's important to be optimistic and encourage her to welcome change, not fear it.

Check out details about the classroom and school. Look for information online or call ahead to help your child get connected quickly with new activities and friends. Younger children don't necessarily want all the information about the new school, but they are often anxious to know about their new classroom. Older children may want to find out everything about teachers, classes, and extracurricular activities.

Just as you would with a child entering school for the first time, help your child become familiar with the schoolgrounds and people she will be meeting before the first day. Organize your own tour, taking in the cafeteria, bathrooms, playground, media center, and physical education area, as well as classrooms.

Get involved. Once your child is attending school, consider volunteering there. This will help your child feel more secure. And be sure to attend parents' nights and teacher conferences.

One of the best things you can do for your child is to let her know that you are there to support her. You might want to set up a specific time each day or each week to debrief with her about her school experience, perhaps by taking a walk together or chatting over a snack. Many parents have found it helpful to share what they experienced as a child and how they coped when they faced a similar situation. And since no two schools have identical curricula, continue to meet with your child's teacher often to make sure your youngster is on track in her new academic program. If your child experiences problems, work with her to help her master school tasks.

Support new and old friendships. Let your home be welcoming; encourage your child to invite any new friends over. Also make the effort to help your child participate when other kids include her in activities or invite her to their homes. Get to know the parents of your child's new friends, too. At the same time, help her maintain contact with old friends. Tell your child she can remember friends from her old school with an album or scrapbook or by putting pictures up in her room. It's easy to stay in touch using email and instant messages—snail mail can be fun, too. Help your child revel in this new adventure and share it with longtime friends as well as new ones!

Making New Friends: Advice from the Experts

These words from other kids might encourage your child:

"I know it sounds silly, but go up to people and say, 'Hi, my name is . . .' to introduce yourself. It really works. I made lots of friends that way!"—Eighth grader, Gaithersburg, MD

"One great idea is to join a club to meet new people."
—Fifth grader, Brooklyn, NY

"Keep an open mind, and don't be always thinking about what things used to be like at your old school and how great your friends were back there. You're not there anymore. Time to put forward a positive outlook!"—Sixth grader, North Potomac, MD

"Ride the school bus if you have a choice. That's a good way to make friends."—Fourth grader, Denver, CO

"Nothing comes in the blink of an eye. I was sad when I moved here from Columbia, but it just takes time. You're going to be okay!"
—Seventh grader, Thousand Oaks, CA

"Keep a diary. It helps to write stuff down, and that way you'll be able to look back at what it was like when you first moved."
—Middle schooler, San Diego, CA

What can you do to prepare your child if you move during the summer?

Some experts say that summer is the best time to move, because it avoids disrupting the school year. Others believe that midyear is a better time, because it lets your child meet other kids right away. You may not have a choice about when you move, but if you do move in the summer, here a few tips to smooth the transition:

- Talk to neighbors right away and get one of them to introduce your child to neighborhood children. Link up with organizations such as Scouts and 4-H.

- Find other ways to help your child make new friends before school starts, perhaps by signing him up for a swimming class. Have him join a youth group through your faith community or other local organizations. Check out the opportunities at the recreation department and community groups, the YMCA or YWCA, or a Boys & Girls Club.

- Meet the school principal and get a list of classes your child will attend and extracurricular activities to choose from so your child can anticipate and prepare.

▥ To make sure your child doesn't feel like a misfit on the first day, ask school staff or other parents about some of the basic cultural norms at school. Do children carry backpacks? Do most students take their own lunches? What about clothing styles? If your child feels like he fits in, he's more likely to stay focused on schoolwork.

How can you help if your child has ongoing problems adjusting?

It may be that you've done everything you can to facilitate a smooth transition, but you can see that your child still looks miserable each morning as she trudges off to school. Not surprisingly, moving is especially stressful for children, who typically have limited coping skills. Many young people need time to adjust to a move. In fact, it may be only after the first month or so that the reality of friends and places left behind finally sinks in, leading your child to begin feeling angry or confused.

Some strategies can help your child at such times:

▥ Remind her that friendships can take a while to develop.

▥ Show understanding by acknowledging both positive and negative feelings. Let her know that it's normal to feel excited about making a new best friend or lonely because of missing an old one and to feel hopeful one day and anxious or discouraged the next.

▥ Let your child know that you, too, have said good-bye to old friends and need to make new ones. Model how to do this.

▥ Demonstrate that your child can maintain contact with old friends just as you do: via mail, email, instant messages, phone calls, and even the occasional small package.

▥ Provide continuity. With everything around being so new, try to maintain the daily routines that your child has been used to. If it's the family tradition to watch Saturday morning cartoons together, start doing that right away in your new home.

▥ Show patience with your child. Even though some children jump head first into new situations and thrive, others need more time (just like adults).

■ Use children's books to help your child come to terms with fears and anxieties about her new situation.

■ If your child continues to have difficulty after several weeks, seek professional help. This can be through the school, your child's healthcare provider, a religious or spiritual advisor, a counseling or social service agency, or a youth leader.

Where can you find out more?

Pages 38–40 include a variety of resources to aid in your search for the right school for your child. Here are other organizations and resources that can be of help with a move or a change of school. National offices are able to link you to services in your local area:

Boys & Girls Clubs of America
1275 Peachtree Street NE
Atlanta, GA 30309
404-487-5700
www.bgca.org

Boy Scouts of America
1325 West Walnut Hill Lane
P.O. Box 152079
Irving, TX 75015
972-580-2401
www.scouting.org

Camp Fire USA
1100 Walnut Street, Suite 1900
Kansas City, MO 64106
816-285-2010
www.campfire.org

Girl Scouts of the USA
420 Fifth Avenue
New York, NY 10018
800-478-7248
www.girlscouts.org

National 4-H
1400 Independence Avenue SW
Washington, DC 20250
202-720-2908
www.4husa.org

Welcome Wagon
245 Newtown Road
Plainview, NY 11803
800-779-3526
www.welcomewagon.com

YMCA of the USA
101 N. Wacker Drive
Chicago, IL 60606
800-872-9622
www.ymca.net

YWCA of the USA
1015 18th Street NW, Suite 1100
Washington, DC 20036
202-467-0801
www.ywca.org

Amber Brown Is Not a Crayon by Paula Danziger (London: Puffin, 2006). Third grader Amber confronts difficult emotions when her best friend moves away. Ages 7–9.

Jack Adrift: Fourth Grade Without a Clue by Jack Gantos (New York: Farrar, Straus and Giroux, 2003). When his father rejoins the Navy and moves the family to Cape Hatteras, North Carolina, 10-year-old Jack becomes confused by a crush on his teacher, contradictory advice from his parents, and a very strange neighbor. Ages 9–12.

Mitchell Is Moving by Marjorie Weinman Sharmat (Pine Plains, NY: Live Oak Media, 1998). A dinosaur's exuberance about moving cools considerably when he realizes how much he misses his next-door friend. Ages 5–8.

My Best Friend Moved Away by Nancy L. Carlson (New York: Viking, 2001). This story eases the pain of saying good-bye, while reassuring young readers that they can make new friends even as they keep old ones close to their hearts. Ages 5–8.

My Name Is Maria Isabel by Alma Flor Ada (New York: Atheneum, 1993). Third grader Maria Isabel, born in Puerto Rico and now living in the United States, wants badly to fit in, and the teacher's writing assignment gives her that opportunity. Ages 7–10.

We Are Best Friends by Aliki (New York: Greenwillow Books, 1982). When his best friend Peter moves away, Robert has no one to play with, no one to fight with, and no fun at all. Then he meets Will and finds he's not the only one who needs a new best friend. Ages 5–8.

We're Moving by Heather Maisner (Boston: Kingfisher, 2004). Amy and her little brother have moved to a new house. They have their own rooms and a big yard to play in. But Amy misses her best friend and the flowers she and Dad planted at their old house. Ages 3–6.

MAKING THE MOST OF THE SCHOOL YEAR

You may have seen the research results indicating that if you are involved in your child's school experiences, he will be far more successful in school and, most likely, in life. But what exactly does this mean?

You know that schoolwork and its related activities are your child's responsibility. It's not your role to write book reports or leave work in the middle of the morning to deliver forgotten assignments. At the same time, you want to support your child's education and school experience and help him develop those critical life skills without which no learning can take place. You can do this at home by showing genuine interest in his work and progress. (I can still recall how thrilled my son, now 22, was when his first-grade poem "Grandma" took center stage on our refrigerator.) You also can structure a home life that is both educationally stimulating and supportive of your child's schoolwork and demonstrate how important education is to you. This chapter answers nitty-gritty questions about the everyday running of your child's school.

How do you develop good communication with your child's teacher?

Staying in touch with your child's teacher is crucial. Teachers need parents' help to do a first-class job. Working together, you and your child's teacher can help your student have a great school year.

While you'll want to meet the teacher early in the year, it's not a good idea to try to do so on the first day. With a barrage of notes from the office and a sea of fresh faces, teachers need time to settle in and to get to know their new charges. If your child is starting kindergarten, you may be invited to come with her on the first day to take part in orientation activities for both of you. This is still not the time for a long personal introduction; save that for a bit later. By waiting a few days to get better acquainted, you also give your child the message that you trust the school and the teacher. This is especially important in the early grades, when Mom or Dad hovering at the classroom door may increase a child's ambivalence about going to school in the first place. If you think your child needs some support, give her a photo of you or some object, like a piece of blanket, to help her feel secure. Then send her into the classroom with a cheerful good-bye, confidently given.

It's critical, of course, that the teacher know early on if your child has any special needs, if there are any serious issues in your child's life such as a new baby or recent death in the family, or if there is a significant health concern such as a problem with bladder control. In most cases you can communicate this ahead of time with a phone call, a note, or an email.

A common practice is for teachers to send home a letter to parents asking questions like these: "What's your child's learning style?" "How do you discipline your child?" "How much TV do you allow your child to watch, and what guidelines do you use?" Even if you do not receive such a request, you can always write your own letter to the teacher. This early written communication can set the stage for face-to-face talks later on. Many teachers, too, are glad to meet parents briefly within a couple of weeks of the start of school.

Virtually all schools have some sort of open house early in the year, and this is another ideal time and place to meet your child's new teacher. At this point, the teacher will typically provide a plan for communicating with parents: for example, a monthly calendar or a weekly letter. Read or listen to the plan carefully, and if something isn't clear, ask questions. Find out how you can get in touch with the teacher at school and exactly when is the best time to call. Be sure to find out if the teacher prefers email or phone communication. Take advantage of this opportunity to get acquainted with the teacher and other parents and become familiar with the classroom environment. If you have a particular issue regarding your child that you want to discuss, make a separate appointment for a later time.

As the year progresses, you will want to maintain parent-teacher communication. Conferences are usually scheduled around grading periods, but don't wait for conference time to let the teacher know when important events are happening for your child or to check in about a troublesome issue. Keeping in touch with the teacher builds a relationship that can be important when concerns arise.

Even if you don't have a particular concern about your child, you can always write a brief note of thanks when the teacher does something that you especially appreciate. Teachers are human—they like to see that someone notices their efforts. As an additional benefit, the opportunity to deliver your note or hear your words of gratitude provides your youngster a first-hand look at the effects of positive, productive communication.

Of course, there is another side to parent involvement: the "helicopter syndrome," in which a parent becomes hyper-involved in every aspect of his or her child's school life. Getting in touch with the teacher because you're concerned that your child doesn't understand his math homework is important and appropriate. Calling, emailing, or text messaging the teacher several times a day pressing for an immediate response is not.

How do you prepare for a parent-teacher conference?

Think of the first conference of the school year as a chance to establish rapport as teammates and figure out how you and the teacher will work together. The conference provides a forum for you to explain your child's strengths, weaknesses, likes, dislikes, interests, and activities, as well as your own special concerns. Equally important, this is your opportunity to hear the teacher's perspective on your child's school performance and interactions with other children.

Many schools schedule a specific time for each conference. If you can't meet at that time, let the teacher know right away and arrange a different time. When you come, be punctual. During the conference, stick to the allotted timeframe; other parents are waiting for the next time slot, and the one after that. The most useful conferences are those in which both teachers and parents stay calm and try hard to work together for one purpose: to help the child do well.

Tips for a Successful Conference

Getting Ready

- Ask your child what he wants you to discuss with the teacher.

- Write down your specific questions and concerns.

- Write down things about your child's life at home. Note information about his personality, habits, and hobbies that you feel is important for the teacher to know.

- Decide on one or two major issues that you want to discuss.

- Be sure to bring paper and pen.

- Arrange for childcare so that you can give your full attention to the conference.

During the Conference

- Begin on a positive note. Thank the teacher for meeting with you. Tell what kind of progress you've noticed and what your child enjoys.

- Refer to your notes so you won't forget important items; take additional notes so that you can share what the teacher has said with your child and family.

- Ask the teacher to show you samples of satisfactory, good, and excellent work, to tell you how this work was evaluated, and to explain how a specific example of your child's work compares with that of other children in the class.

- Ask if your child is working at grade level and what expectations the teacher has.

- Check into your child's social skills. Does he play with others? Spend time alone?

- Ask for an explanation if the teacher says something you don't quite understand.

- Restate important points the teacher makes to be sure you avoid miscommunication.

- You may not always agree with the teacher. When this happens, respectfully say that you disagree but that you want to continue cooperating to explore the issue further.

- Write down any plans or activities you develop together to improve your child's academic performance or behavior. Leave with a plan of action.

- Let the teacher know how to reach you, and be certain that you know how to report back or check in.

Following Up

- Discuss the conference with your child so he knows what you've learned and how you plan to work with the teacher.

- Share any compliments the teacher has offered about your child. Keep a positive tone, even when talking about a problem.

- Follow through at home, as you have agreed to do.

- Stay in regular communication with the teacher, and get in touch when you need more information on your child's academic progress.

- If you are not satisfied with the teacher's responses, do not hesitate to schedule a meeting with the principal. Remember: you are your child's best advocate.

While the standard format for the parent-teacher conference is still the norm in the fall, some schools are using a different model for the spring meeting: the student-led conference. Here, students show parents some of their work and explain their grades. The idea is that with the child leading the conference, he will be able to communicate not only how he is doing, but why.

What are the best ways to be involved in your child's school and classroom?

A good way to answer this question is to ask yourself another: "What can I give and what do I want to get?" If your answer indicates that you think you can be of help to the instructional program, and you like the satisfaction that working with groups of children gives you, you might consider volunteering as a classroom aide or after-school tutor. On the other hand, if your answer indicates that you are more of a political person and you want to influence how the school functions, consider serving on one of the many school committees open to parents. In other words, choose something you truly care about and are comfortable doing. Also take into account practical considerations. Be sure to evaluate where your skills lie and how many hours you can devote to volunteering so that you can make the best use of your available time.

If you decide to volunteer in the classroom, you'll find that most teachers will welcome you with open arms. Your presence in the classroom may allow a teacher to break the class into small reading groups in which every child has a chance to read aloud to an adult. Or, depending on your skills and interest, a teacher might be able to rely on you to work in the computer lab or media center or to offer students assistance with music or art projects.

If you are a parent who works outside the home, find out if your employer will allow you flex time to volunteer at your child's school. If such an arrangement isn't feasible, consider other options. Some teachers, for example, have projects that parents can help prepare at home. Likewise, you may be able to aid your child's school by soliciting community donations or inviting local businesses, including your employer, to become active in supporting the school. Businesses recognize that supporting educational efforts demonstrates and builds citizenship and makes for great publicity, too.

Your first grader might love having Dad or Mom in the classroom, but your seventh grader may worry that you are invading her territory. Whether they show it or not, most children are proud that their parents care enough to give of themselves at their school. Keep in mind that volunteering doesn't have to be limited to your child's classroom. Indeed, as your child gets older, many other service opportunities will appear: working in the student store, sponsoring the band, assistant coaching a sports team, assisting with a theatrical or art project, helping at the concession stand at sports events—the list goes on.

> ### Part of the Team
>
> The father of a fourth grader in Pasadena, California, says that spending an hour a week in his son's class helping with math answered every question he had about his son's classwork. He learned to trust his son's teacher and became more willing to listen to her observations about his son. This dad's classroom volunteering gave him firsthand evidence of something every teacher wishes parents understood: the child at school can be very different from the child at home.

 ## How can you evaluate your child's teacher?

Teachers choose their work because they love children and they love learning, yet these qualities alone will not ensure that your child has a first-rate teacher. In evaluating your child's teacher, make sure first that he or she is trained and credentialed and second that the school administration values the teacher as a professional. Quality teachers and teaching are the fruit of a supportive school environment. (For more on what makes a good school environment, see pages 25–27.)

In addition, it's important for your child's teacher to:

- Show knowledge and excitement about the subject matter and encourage your child's interest and enthusiasm for learning, making it both enjoyable and stimulating.

- Challenge your child academically and hold high expectations for his ability to learn. Expect the teacher to help your child understand what he needs to learn, encourage him to work hard, and give him clear feedback on his academic progress.

- Maintain a classroom in which everyone is treated with courtesy and respect. An effective teacher establishes order without being oppressive and treats all students fairly.

- Organize the classroom to make effective use of children's time. Students should know what they are supposed to be doing and should be actively involved in learning.

- Possess strong diagnostic skills in order to determine what your child knows and teach him what he needs to learn. By assessing your child often enough, the teacher should be aware of knowledge and skills your child has acquired and be able to follow a plan to help him progress.

- Emphasize self-assessment so that students don't just rely on grades to know how they're doing. The teacher should help your child be able to recognize when he does or doesn't understand something and to ask for help as necessary.

- Communicate regularly with parents and alert them promptly if there is any cause for concern. You want the teacher to give you clear information about what your child is supposed to learn and about his success in learning those things.

Of course, it's not reasonable to expect your child's teacher to demonstrate these qualities five days a week, 180 days a year. Like the rest of the world, teachers have good days and bad. Classroom teachers also face unique pressures and often-unpredictable conditions: They interact daily with upwards of twenty to thirty lively minds and bodies. They are called on to deal on the spot with a host of personal, social, and physical concerns and to help children cope with the news of national and international crises and natural disasters. A good teacher will maintain high standards and goals regardless of the challenges and will remain generally optimistic and energetic.

If you have misgivings or concerns about a teacher, seek more information and input. Talk to other parents, to your child and his friends, and maybe even to the school principal. Know, too, that not every teacher clicks with every student. Even the best teacher can have a style or personality that rubs a child or parent the wrong way. In a case like this, don't jump headfirst into trying to remove your child from the class. An experienced and capable teacher may recognize the situation and be able to prevent a personality issue from getting in the way of teaching and learning.

The teacher's job is to *teach*—not to be liked. Parents can help children understand that even if a teacher is not to their liking, this is still someone they can learn from. At some point over the course of twelve or thirteen years, your child will more than likely face this situation. Encourage your child to focus on the positive, do his best, and get what he can out of the class.

That said, if you continually hear from your child and from parents or other children that the teacher treats the class disrespectfully, consistently puts down students in front of the group, allows the students to run wild so that they're not safe, or teaches inappropriate material, then you need to take action. These are signs of a problem teacher, and it's critical that you address the matter with the principal promptly. You have the right to request that your child be removed from the class.

Can you request a particular teacher?

Most schools do not officially offer parents the opportunity to select their child's teacher. School policies may mildly discourage this, or they may have a firm rule against fulfilling these requests.

What if you think it's important that your child have a particular teacher? If your child's school is one where your request is likely to be well received, then ask for the teacher you want. Do this early, preferably in the spring when classroom assignments are being made. Appeal to the principal, school counselor, or school psychologist and describe how your child's learning style would benefit from being matched with a teacher with similar strengths. In other words, emphasize the positive. If you can't arrange a meeting in person, write a letter that points out what you feel your child needs in school: for example, a very orderly classroom with traditional instruction and not much free time. Then ask that your child be assigned to the teacher you believe will satisfy those needs.

Make a strong case for your child, and then let it be. Some administrators will weigh and honor these requests if they are able to; some may have sound reasons why they cannot do so. Either way, you don't want to gain a reputation as a pesky parent and end up finding that school personnel are increasingly unavailable to meet with you on other issues. Principals, along with teachers and counselors, put a good deal of time and care into the selection of students for each class. They consider class makeup as well as individual compatibility with the teacher. School administrators want to create the best possible learning environment for each student. They work hard to take into account a number of academic and social factors, all the while seeking to establish balanced classes.

How can you find out the school's and teacher's policies on behavior and discipline?

In general, a school discipline policy is designed to guarantee the safety of students and staff, create an effective learning environment, foster respect for others, and teach students how to resolve conflicts.

In most cases, discipline policies are decided at the school level. Each individual school is required to have a written discipline code. This code, which describes students' rights and responsibilities, should be available on your school's Web site or in printed form. As with other areas of your child's education, it's a good idea to check out your school's discipline policy early on. Don't wait until your child is summoned to the principal's office.

Carefully examine the policy. Make sure it states clearly what behavior is expected of a student. Check what reinforcements and consequences are established for acceptable and unacceptable behavior. You'll also want to see what level of parental involvement is expected. Discipline policies often require parents to share responsibility for their children's behavior at school. This means letting your child know what you expect of her, coming to school for conferences, and helping your child understand that rules must be made and enforced for the good of all the students. You may be asked to sign a form indicating that you have discussed the school's expectations with your child and that you promise to review these regularly.

While the overall school discipline policy sets the foundation, every teacher also needs to build a sense of order, respect, and trust in the classroom. Educators may use a variety of techniques to do this, depending on the individual teacher and the grade level. Proven techniques include having students come up with class rules and consequences, always waiting for complete silence before beginning a class, focusing on praising good behavior rather than giving too much attention to inappropriate behavior, and if necessary, contacting parents to alert them to classroom misbehavior.

Over time, teachers discover what methods work best for them. Good teachers know that establishing behavior expectations along with consequences for not meeting those expectations is crucial in the first week of school. They know that if clear rules are not in place early on, the business of teaching and learning cannot take place. Your child's teacher most likely will explain the class discipline policy to you in an introductory letter or at a back-to-school open house. If you don't receive this important information early in the school year, don't hesitate to ask for it. As long as the policy seems reasonable to you, be willing to back up the teacher as necessary.

How much homework should your child be expected to complete?

Parents differ on the subject of how much schoolwork they'd like their children to bring home each day. Teacher attitudes differ as well. Evidence suggests that the right amount of homework, designed appropriately for a child's developmental level, does promote learning. As a general rule of thumb, the National Education Association (NEA) and the national Parent Teacher Association (PTA) suggest starting with ten minutes of homework per night in first grade and incrementally adding ten minutes with each grade level. Thus, a second grader should be assigned twenty minutes of homework, a third grader thirty minutes, a fourth grader forty minutes, and so on—not to exceed two hours per night in high school. More often than not, homework overload is an exercise in futility, because the student can feel overwhelmed by the sheer quantity of work, become distracted or bored, and end up making a halfhearted effort just to get it done.

Harris Cooper, Ph.D., a professor and director of education at Duke University, has reviewed over a hundred studies on the effectiveness of homework. In general, he has found that the benefits of doing homework seem to depend on the student's grade level. In high school, students who regularly do homework outperform those who do not, as measured by standardized tests and grades. In middle school, homework is half as effective, and in elementary school, it has no apparent measurable effect on achievement. Still, homework at the elementary level is important and has a potentially long-term impact: it helps younger children form effective study skills, which in turn influence grades and successful learning.

Homework needs to reinforce what happens in the classroom, not teach new material or supplant classwork. A Spanish-language teacher in Oak Park, California, likens teachers and students to sports coaches and players: while players can go out and practice on their own hour after hour, the best learning occurs when the coach is right there, explaining and demonstrating new plays and skills and immediately correcting any flaws.

How can you help your child with homework?

In terms of homework, you can expect to work with your child quite a bit when he is in first or second grade, but by fourth grade, it's reasonable for him to be doing the work himself and then having you check it. Once he's in fifth grade, your role is to be more of a supervisor. Some children may still need their parent close by, not necessarily for help, but just as a supportive presence.

What if you see that your child is having trouble with homework? Resist the urge to rush in and rescue or reprimand. Rather, begin by figuring out exactly what's going on. Check if your child is writing down the assignment correctly, bringing his assignment book home, and getting the finished work into his backpack to return to class. If he's simply not doing the work, find out why. Is your child struggling because the work is too difficult? Does he seem to have too much homework or not enough? Let the teacher know the situation.

Doing homework gives your child an opportunity to develop responsibility and self-discipline. Remembering assignments, organizing materials, gathering information, and budgeting time are important skills your child will need throughout life.

Hassle-Free Homework: Eight Tools of the Trade

1. **A routine.** Set a pattern for yourself and your child—for example, half an hour of downtime after school followed by a snack, homework, then dinner at six. Or maybe homework takes place after supper. The point is to plan a routine that works for you and your child and keep it consistent.

2. **A place.** Arrange a comfortable place for your child to do homework, such as in his room, at the kitchen table, or in a quiet corner of the living room.

3. **Parameters for your child.** Ensure that your child has every-thing he needs to be productive. Some children really do work better if they are listening to music, although *not* with the television on.

4. **Parameters for you.** Ask teachers about their homework policies. How much time should the homework take? How much involvement from parents does the teacher expect?

5. **Role modeling.** Set a good example. Children are more moti-vated to do homework when they see parents doing home-work, too. Sit down and go through the mail, pay bills, read, or catch up on correspondence.

6. **Tools.** Provide supplies and resources—pencils, pens, paper, an assignment book, and a dictionary. Keep everything together in one place.

7. **Ongoing interest.** Show an interest. Ask your child about class topics and assignments. Post long-term projects on the refrig-erator. Attend school activities. Be available for questions.

8. **Appropriate help.** Monitor homework. Help your child under-stand assignments, get organized, and structure time, but do not do the work for him.

What programs are offered outside of the regular school day?

More and more public schools are providing programming beyond the school day. The programs are known by various names: after-school, extended-day, school-age childcare, and expanded learning are a few examples. Not all programs are the same, but whatever their focus, they offer some common benefits. Effective supple-mental programs can:

- Improve your child's grades and attitudes about learning.

- Give your child an opportunity to make new friends.

- Lessen your worries when you cannot be with your child before or after school.

▦ Involve entire communities in the enrichment of your child.

▦ Prevent risky behaviors.

Due to grants and subsidies from local foundations and business or civic groups, many schools are able to offer extended-day programs at no cost. Where there is a fee involved, financial assistance based on a sliding scale can often be arranged, so if you are concerned about costs, ask about such options.

To find out what programming your child's school offers, check with the teacher or principal. If there are no extra programs at the school, look into those sponsored by community organizations such as the YMCA, Boys & Girls Clubs, scouting groups, your local park and recreation department, or police athletic leagues. Talk to other families about what their children do before and after school.

The programs you find will have a variety of offerings including, but not limited to, homework help and tutoring, study time and enrichment activities, performing and visual arts lessons and opportunities (music, drama, painting), and sports. Visit a program yourself to determine its quality and whether it is the right opportunity for your child.

Evaluating an After-School Program: A Checklist

Here's a quick checklist of what to look for and ask about in a supplemental program:

☑ Are all staff members well qualified to work with children?

☑ Are background checks routinely carried out before staff members are hired?

☑ Will the program director readily supply references so that you can speak with parents of children currently enrolled?

☑ Does the staff have a system to determine where the children are at all times? What other provisions are in place to ensure children's safety?

☑ What discipline procedures are followed?

☑ Are there enough staff members to allow children the opportunity for one-on-one adult attention?

☑ Does the staff make children feel welcome and comfortable? Do the children seem happy, stimulated, and well supervised?

☑ Are children engaged in learning activities through computers, the arts, special projects, or homework help? Are the activities well suited to children's ages?

☑ Do children have the opportunity to choose what they will do, how they will do it, and with whom?

☑ Are the facilities clean and in good shape? Is there enough physical space for children to comfortably take part in a range of activities?

☑ Does the program encourage the involvement of parents and others in the community? Are there adult helpers, tutors, and mentors?

How do you enroll your child in extracurricular activities?

Depending on its size, your child's school may offer a broad range of extracurricular activities. In most cases, you will need to fill out an application for after-school club participation; there may be a fee. To sign up or obtain an application, call or visit the school or go online to the school's Web site. In general, students are admitted to extracurricular activities on a first-come, first-served basis, so it may be a good idea for your child to decide which activity she'd like to take part in and to enroll as early as possible.

While your elementary school child is unlikely to face many official rules for eligibility, there may be age or interest guidelines or other considerations. For middle schoolers, involvement in school-sponsored extracurricular activities will most likely depend on maintaining a set grade point average (GPA) and adhering to the program's rules and expectations.

Are extracurricular activities a good idea? As with so much of life, the key is balance. Since schoolwork is your child's top priority, don't hesitate to make continued participation in sports or clubs contingent upon maintaining an agreed-upon standard of academic performance. Another issue is overscheduling. While structured activities can teach discipline and goal setting, too many commitments can simply exhaust both your child and you. Children need time for informal socializing as well as downtime to be alone, relax, entertain themselves, and just enjoy being kids.

Is your school doing all it can to keep your child safe?

If you were to judge solely by the evening news, you might conclude that school violence is dramatically on the rise. According to a report issued by the United States Department of Education, however, such is not the case.[1] Despite the incidents of school violence that capture media attention, the reality is that your child is safer in school than almost anywhere else in the community, due to the high degree of supervision that schools provide. It's also true that the majority of schoolchildren are rule-abiding students who want to learn.

There are two key components to a sound school safety policy: philosophy and practice. Cultivating a school atmosphere in which every student feels welcome is key to a school safety policy. The specifics of the plan are also important and should cover in detail your school's approach to preventing disruptive and inappropriate behavior, intervening when it happens, and responding to a crisis. A proactive safety plan in which everyone knows what to do in time of a crisis is crucial.

Principals want to make their schools as safe as they can be, and each individual school designs different measures to provide for building security. Many schools keep their exterior doors locked during regular school hours, requiring visitors to enter through a main door, sign in at the office, and receive a visitor's badge. Your child's school undoubtedly has safety drills; other measures may include surveillance cameras, locker and backpack checks, metal detectors, or even the presence of police officers.

Questions to Ask School Staff About Safety

Prevention

- What type of proactive safety plan does the school have in place?

- Can I see the plan?

- Does the school conduct trial runs to make sure the plan works?

- What means of conflict resolution does the school have in place for dealing with disagreements between students?

- What can I do to ensure that the school is safe for my child?

Intervention

- How do staff members intervene when they see disturbing behaviors such as frequent angry outbursts, fighting, or bullying?

- Are teachers and counselors trained to recognize early warning signs of depression?

- Do teachers and administrators sit down and talk with students when they see inappropriate behavior?

Crisis Response

- If there is a crisis situation at school, what procedures are parents to follow?

- Is there a particular area designated as a pickup place in case of an emergency?

- Do the students know what to do?

- Does the school have a liaison with other organizations such as the fire department, the sheriff's office, and bus drivers to coordinate in time of emergency?

Finally, consider: Does your child's school have emergency contact information and procedures for your family? Have you talked to your child about these procedures?

Many schools also have a *zero tolerance* policy, which means that particular types of misconduct are simply not tolerated and specific consequences or interventions are established as policy and applied in all cases. There is some controversy around zero tolerance, and schools vary in the ways they implement and enforce it. For example, a student bringing a firearm to school is clearly not to be tolerated, but what if a child brings a toy that appears to be a weapon, such as a plastic knife? In many schools, this could be grounds for suspension. Be sure to check out your school's policy, especially regarding what is acceptable for your child to bring to school and what is not.

It may be that your concern about safety at school is much more immediate. Perhaps your child has come home complaining that he's afraid to get on the school bus because some of the students are pushing him around or that the bathrooms at school always have water on the floor and door locks that don't work. In cases like this, contact the school principal immediately by phone or email. Chances are your principal will be grateful for having been alerted to a possibly explosive situation.

A safe school is one that responds to any threat to its security with confidence and as a whole community. In a safe school, students and staff walk with eyes forward, not looking over their shoulders either literally or figuratively. They feel secure and comfortable in their surroundings. There is an absence of conflict between teachers and principals, parents and staff, students and staff. In a safe school, all the parties are working together to be and stay safe.

What can you do if your child is being bullied at school?

Bullying can be physical (hitting, shoving, kicking), verbal (put-downs, name-calling, bigoted remarks), or relational (spreading rumors, making threats, leaving someone out). When it comes to detecting bullying, parents often run into a puzzling phenomenon: silence. A parent may sense that a youngster is having a problem, but the child may not say anything about it directly. Here are some indicators that your child may be experiencing a problem with bullying or harassment:

- unexplained injuries, scratches, or torn clothing
- reluctance to go to school or ride the bus
- irritability and refusal to say what's wrong
- sleeplessness or loss of appetite
- frequent headaches and other physical complaints
- requests for "protection"
- sudden changes in school performance, relationships, or mood

This list is not exhaustive. And although there could be other explanations for these behaviors, they are common signs of bullying, so if you suspect it, find a private opportunity to talk calmly with your child. Learn as much as you can about what has occurred. Make notes of who was involved, what happened, and when and where it took place. Then contact the school right away and arrange to meet with the teacher and the principal. Give them your written record and determine exactly what the teacher, the school, you, and your child can do to protect your child and stop the bullying.

Tattling vs. Telling

Many outbursts of school violence are related directly or indirectly to retaliation for bullying, so it is extremely important for you to sit down and talk with your child about bullying behavior. Start by defining what you mean by this: bullying happens when a person or group of people makes another person feel hurt, afraid, or uncomfortable on purpose over and over again. Ask your child if there is anyone at school she is afraid of. Find out what she would do if she were threatened. Let your child know that keeping bullying to herself and hoping that it will go away just doesn't work. Help your child see that when a situation is dangerous, telling an adult about it is not tattling. One way to explain the distinction is this: Tattling gets someone *in* trouble; telling is the only way to get someone *out* of trouble.

The school has a responsibility to deal with bullying that occurs on school property and, in many cases, between school and home, and you can expect your child's teacher or administrator to do several things:

- Step in and stop it immediately.

- Remove the audience (other students) from the scene.

- Act promptly in talking to the victim and the bully, and do so separately.

- Contact the parents or guardians of the bully and the victim.

- Communicate with other teachers and administrators to share insights.

- Maintain communication with parents until the situation is resolved.

While you may need some patience as school officials work to resolve the situation, monitor how things are going and talk to school officials again if you see continuing problems. Through all this, try to stay calm for your child's sake. Assure her that working together with the school, you and she will be able to take care of this situation. Let her know that you will make sure her school follows up and puts an end to it. At the same time, tell your child that this is not supposed to happen and that she does not deserve it. And instruct her that the way to fight back is to inform the school authorities about what happened and *not* to fight or hurt someone back, no matter how tempting it may be.

"Bully proof" your child so that she will be able to deal with any future incidents. This means teaching her appropriate assertiveness skills: how to stand and walk with confidence, how to express feelings clearly, how to speak up for herself assertively and not aggressively, and how to say no when feeling uncomfortable or pressured by others. In addition, help your child build skills for making and keeping friends. Teach her to walk away and get adult help when confronted by a dangerous situation. A great idea, which many parents have used successfully, is to act out such situations and have your child practice responses through role playing.

Bullying is a serious and widespread problem that should never be dismissed as "Boys will be boys" or "That's how girls treat each other." Bullying is *not* a normal part of growing up; in fact, it's a serious social problem. According to the National School Safety Center (NSSC), one in seven children becomes a victim of bullying at school.[2] In recent years, many schools have developed antibullying programs, generally designed to teach students about respect and conflict resolution and to train them in specific actions to take when they experience, witness, or know about bullying.

? What can you do if you think your child is bullying others?

Perhaps you suspect, but are not sure, that your child is bullying someone else. You may have noticed that your child pushes boundaries, behaves aggressively at home, has trouble losing, seems to enjoy other people's discomfort, or finds it hard to empathize—all possible signs that a child bullies or could bully others. If so, make an extra effort to show interest in your child's relationships and to encourage him to talk about strong feelings. Research has shown that violent "screen time" impacts children negatively, so keep a close watch on the content of TV shows, computer and video games, and movies, as well as the amount of time spent with them. Set reasonable limits in other areas as well. Take time to help your child develop social skills—confident and respectful ways to interact with other children and adults. The teacher or school counselor may be able to suggest a program that teaches ways to manage anger and resolve conflicts.

What if you *know* your child is bullying someone? Even if he denies it, make sure your child hears from you that bullying is not acceptable. Set an appointment to talk with the teacher and other school officials as well; get information, enlist their support, and arrange a way to stay in touch about how your child is doing. At home, use reasonable discipline. It's natural to feel frustrated as a parent, but take care not to yell, make threats, or treat your child coldly. These actions are similar to the hurtful behaviors you want to discourage and will send a confusing message. Perhaps most important, show your child that you believe in him and will not give up on working together to help him learn to get along better with others.

What is the benefit of joining a parent organization?

Almost every school has some sort of parent organization. It can be an invaluable source of information and support. There's nothing like getting advice on navigating your child's school from parents who have already learned the ropes. A school's parent organization may be an informal group of involved parents or a formally established Parent Teacher Association (PTA) or Parent Teacher Organization (PTO).

Parent Teacher Associations. PTAs are local groups that affiliate with the national PTA, which was founded in 1897. These groups pay dues to their respective state PTAs and to the national PTA. In return, they receive member benefits and a voice in the operations of the larger organization. At the national level, the PTA supports and speaks on behalf of children both in schools and before governmental bodies and other organizations that make decisions affecting young people. It also works to encourage parent involvement in our public schools. The national PTA's Web site (www.pta.org) is a rich resource for parents, providing information on topics from student achievement to media technology to health and wellness.

Parent Teacher Organizations. PTO is a more general term, representing the thousands of groups that choose to remain independent of the PTA. Many such groups take the name PTO, although you may also find PCC (Parent Communication Council), PTG (Parent-Teacher Group), and HAS (Home and School Association). These are usually single-school groups operating under their own bylaws and working for their individual school or community. As with PTAs, the overall goal of all these groups is to build strong, nurturing schools, support children's educational and social needs, encourage parent and community involvement in public and private schools, and bring together parents and teachers in a mutual cooperation.

By definition, your PTA or PTO provides a key opportunity for you to directly influence your child's school and education.

Parents with a Purpose

When Rooney Ranch Elementary School in Lakewood, Colorado, lost its crossing guards, the parent organization went to work. They talked to people in the neighborhood, including those who didn't have school-age children. They approached people who lived near corners, where crossing guards were needed. And they succeeded in getting a complete crossing guard enterprise up and running, covering forty sites near the school and involving the entire community.

————

In San Francisco, with the support of the local chapter of the PTA, parents were able to save arts programs for their elementary schools by establishing a task force and holding public hearings. Their efforts led to a solution in which the City of San Francisco stepped in to provide the needed programming funds.

Your participation shows your child that you care about education. And your involvement, combined with that of other parents, can have a far-reaching impact. Whatever you give your child and community, sooner or later you will get it back.

Where can you find out more?

Page 62 includes a variety of resources to aid in your search for before- and after-school programming, including scouting organizations, Boys & Girls Clubs, 4-H, and YMCA/YWCA. Pages 18–20 list additional information about PTA, PTO, PTO Today, and Parents for Public Schools (PPS). Here are additional resources to help you make the most of the school year:

The Bully, the Bullied, and the Bystander by Barbara Coloroso (New York: HarperCollins, 2003). This book for parents, teachers, and other adults concerned about bullying offers ideas for empowering children against mistreatment.

Charles Stewart Mott Foundation
503 S. Saginaw Street, Suite 1200
Flint, MI 48502
810-238-5651
www.mott.org
This foundation is a leading partner in the U.S. Department of Education's 21st Century Community Learning Centers initiative that supports local after-school programs.

The End of Homework: How Homework Disrupts Families, Overburdens Children, and Limits Learning by Etta Kralovec and John Buell (Boston: Beacon Press, 2000). A fresh and thought-provoking look at the homework debate.

The Essential Conversation: What Parents and Teachers Can Learn from Each Other by Sara Lawrence-Lightfoot (New York: Random House, 2003). A very helpful book for any parent or teacher who wants to get the most out of their relationship in the interest of children.

Family Education Network
501 Boylston Street, Suite 900
Boston, MA 02116
617-671-2000
www.familyeducation.com
The Web site provides many links for parents that offer grade-specific advice for school success.

Get Organized Without Losing It by Janet S. Fox (Minneapolis: Free Spirit Publishing, 2006). A humorous, helpful book for kids ages 8–13 that offers great information on how to organize all school-related aspects of their life—a good book to read with your child.

How to Help Your Child with Homework by Jeanne Shay Schumm (Minneapolis: Free Spirit Publishing, 2005). This comprehensive and informative guide features practical advice for parents on encouraging good study habits and ending the "homework wars."

In Schools We Trust: Creating Communities of Learning in an Era of Testing and Standardization by Deborah Meier (Boston: Beacon Press, 2002). The author, a founder of nationally acclaimed small public schools in Boston and New York, discusses the value of small schools where teachers, students, and parents know one another well.

National Alliance for Safe Schools (NASS)
Ice Mountain
P.O. Box 290
Slanesville, WV 25444-0290
304-496-8100
www.safeschools.org
NASS works to ensure all schools have an active plan for creating and maintaining a healthy and safe environment for students and faculty.

National School Safety Center (NSSC)
141 Duesenberg Drive, Suite 11
Westlake Village, CA 91362
805-373-9977
www.schoolsafety.us
This center provides useful resources on how to create safe schools and how to deal with bullying, as well as information on school safety training and products.

Speak Up and Get Along! by Scott Cooper (Minneapolis: Free Spirit Publishing, 2005). Written for children ages 8–12, this book teaches kids how to build social skills and deal with bullying. It includes lots of dialogue lines and skills practice along with information for parents.

Chapter Notes

1. U.S. Department of Education, "Violent Crime Rate Against Students Drops, New Report Says," press release, November 2004.

2. National School Safety Center, "Bullying in Schools, Bullying Fact Sheet Series: Fighting the Bully Battle," 2006, p. 3.

THE CONNECTED CLASSROOM AND THE WIRED SCHOOL

There's no doubt about it: computers and the Internet are now an established part of your child's education. Today nearly 100 percent of public schools in the United States have Internet access. As of 2005, the ratio of public school students to Internet-equipped instructional computers was about four students per computer.[1] In some regions and districts the ratio is as low as one-to-one, as schools explore the idea of providing every student with a laptop.

Schools are also using their Internet access more frequently to build school Web sites that can offer anything from lunch menus to online practice tests and daily homework assignments. In what may prove to be the way testing is conducted in the future, twenty-one states and the District of Columbia offered computer-based assessment in the 2005–06 school year.[2] There's also the growing phenomenon of virtual schools, where instruction takes place over the Internet rather than in a traditional classroom setting. More than half the states have a state-established virtual school or at least one cyber charter school.[3] You may be wondering if all this technology is really a good thing and what it means for your child. Chapter 6 looks at some of the issues around computer use in schools today.

Are computers good for your child?

Learning via computer technology is a fairly new phenomenon, and there isn't any research yet to prove conclusively how and to what extent computers enhance learning. The ways in which they're used vary widely from teacher to teacher, subject to subject, and school to school. That said, computers can motivate students, including those who have previously been turned off about learning. Technology provides new types of educational experiences and allows teaching to be tailored to the strengths and needs of the individual child. Children have differing learning styles, and a child who learns best visually or spatially, for example, may find the computer especially useful. Computers also allow teachers to present materials from nearly all subject areas in a variety of ways.

How Do Kids Use Computers in School?

Here's a sample of some tech lessons your child might encounter in a typical week:

- **Vocabulary building.** Using a print or an online dictionary, children can work in groups to define a set of words the teacher has written on the board, create a crossword puzzle with a software program, and finally share the puzzle with other classmates.

- **Spelling and math.** Numerous programs allow children to customize their math or spelling and then provide instant feedback on their responses, so that students actually have a kind of dialogue with the program.

- **Math baseball.** Choosing +, –, ×, or /, and selecting a level of difficulty (easy, medium, hard, or super brain), a child can see how many "runs" she can score by solving math problems before getting three outs (making three problem errors).

- **Geography.** Children can use online maps to locate their country and state, pinpoint their home address, and get directions from home to school or another location.

- **Creative writing and drawing.** After listening to a read-aloud story, children can compose their own original endings or use drawing software to illustrate what they want to happen at the end of the story.

- **Essay writing.** At many schools, pencil and paper have become things of the past as students complete assignments online. Using special software, children are able to identify grammar and spelling errors and correct them before submitting their essays to the teacher. The teacher in turn can use a highlighter feature to point out any errors, make comments, and return the essays to students—all online.

Parents and teachers alike testify to the benefits of computer-based learning for all students. Computers can help your child raise her test scores, provided that the software specifically targets certain skills and your child's teacher knows how to use it. Children with learning differences benefit enormously from a computer, which can be a great help in learning spelling, developing numerical abilities, and also with organizational skills. A child with dyslexia, who may have trouble keeping more than one idea or direction in her head at one time, can easily view several ideas on the screen at the same time and visually organize them.

At the same time, while technology is *a* learning tool, it's not the *only* one. Although students can use a computer to do Internet research, acquire basic skills, solve countless problems, and learn interactively, the computer can produce only the information a student asks for. If the students have not received adequate instruction in the proper use of computers, or if the software is uninspiring, then computers are less helpful and can even be harmful. And computers can't teach students how to think. A well-rounded education should include many other tools, such as cooperative learning in groups, peer interaction, projects, field trips, experiential and hands-on learning, and the use of books, magazines, and other visuals.

Of course, it doesn't matter how many Internet-connected computers are in your child's school if teachers are not trained to use them. A majority of states have standards for what teachers should know about technology, but only twenty-one require teachers to demonstrate technology proficiency before receiving an initial license, either by completing coursework or passing a test.[4]

When used effectively, computers have a role to play in helping your child learn. It is important, too, for children to be able to navigate through basic computer applications. They will need the skills as their school careers progress. Most high schools today require at least one technology credit for graduation, and almost all states have technology standards in place, outlining what students should be able to do by the end of high school in preparation for postsecondary education and the world of work.

What are the advantages of the Internet for your child?

Perhaps the most compelling feature of the wired classroom is that, via the Internet and the World Wide Web, it brings millions of resources together in one place, something that no other medium can do. Every student can become a modern-day explorer and set out on his own voyage of discovery on the Web. It doesn't matter where your school is located. One elementary school art teacher noted: "At one point I was teaching in a small school in rural Montana, and with the Internet, my students had the same opportunities to view art as the kids in New York City." Additional examples range across the curriculum:

- When an art student wants to draw a hippopotamus, he can simply type "hippo" in the search box and he'll have his model in thirty seconds or less.

- Foreign-language classes can explore up-to-date newspapers and museums located in other countries, resources they couldn't readily find on the shelves of their local library.

- Historical information is at students' fingertips. A technology director at a middle school in Brooklyn, New York, reported using a site that had all the data from every U.S. Census that have ever been recorded. She described a project where students take statistics from the North and the South before the Civil War, compare facts, and draw conclusions about the causes of the war.

In addition, the Internet facilitates online collaboration among students. In one project, students around the U.S. worked together to monitor levels of acid rain. Your child may well be involved in a program such as MayaQuest, which connects teachers and students with explorers and scientists in Belize as they explore why the Mayan civilization collapsed. Every day for two weeks, students "talk" to the experts via email and watch them as they make their way on bikes through the country, speaking with scholars and visiting ruins.

Your child can also reap the benefit if his teacher takes advantage of the wide range of materials available on the Internet in preparing classes. Numerous Web sites offer not only lesson plans but also a range of how-to resources. Creating a mural for the school, for instance, becomes easy when the teacher can go online to find information about the process and contact people who have designed murals. The Internet makes it easy for teachers to interact with one another, create a community, and share ideas, all of which are particularly helpful if your child happens to attend a school that's small or isolated. Another plus teachers have reported is that since students enjoy using the Internet, classroom management issues do not arise so often, allowing for more uninterrupted learning time.

What about the Internet's downside?

Along with access to a world of information come risks related to accuracy of information, appropriateness of content, student safety, the potential for plagiarism, and use of time. Students, teachers, schools, and parents all have a role to play in knowing and avoiding the potential pitfalls.

Reliability of online sources. Information obtained on the Internet is only useful if your child has training in how to evaluate the credibility of her sources. Since people can publish whatever they choose online, it's important for your child to understand that the Internet is simply a vehicle for distributing information—it offers no guarantee of accuracy. Children must be taught media literacy and know how to recognize misinformation.

Many school librarians have developed Internet checklists, which students are required to fill out to determine the credibility of an Internet source before they can use it. A typical checklist looks something like this:

- ☑ Who is the author? Are the author's credentials stated?
- ☑ Who is the sponsor of the site? Is there an organization affiliated with the site or its author?
- ☑ Is the material free of error (typos, spelling, grammar)?
- ☑ Are the sources for factual information in the material clearly identified? Can you verify them?
- ☑ Is any bias present?
- ☑ To what extent is the material meant to persuade? Is this clearly stated?
- ☑ Is the page an advertisement or some other kind of promotional material?
- ☑ Who is the intended audience?
- ☑ When was the site last updated? Does it rely on the most current available information? If not, is the reason clearly stated and justified?

It's also common for schools to subscribe to reputable, professionally screened databases where teachers can direct their students, confident that the information is credible.

Safe, appropriate viewing. If you are worried about the appropriateness of what your child may be viewing, find out if the school has online filters in place to protect the students from certain kinds of material. Under the Children's Internet Protection Act (CIPA), a federal law passed in 2001, any school or library that receives discounted rates for Internet access, Internet service, or internal connections must develop an Internet safety policy and use technology protection measures that block or filter Internet access to material that is obscene, pornographic, or otherwise harmful to minors. This means that filtering is now required by law for elementary and secondary schools. As an extra precaution, you also may be asked to sign a paper giving permission for your child to use the Internet.

Potential for plagiarism. Teachers report that the biggest downside of student Internet use is plagiarism. Many teachers note that it's just far too easy for students to take somebody else's work, intentionally or not, and teachers and schools are learning that they have to teach students what plagiarism is and why it's wrong. A middle school teacher in Montana explains, "Half the time my students don't understand the difference between getting research online before putting it into your own words and just plain copying everything you find." With cut-and-paste computer commands, a student can quickly put together a paper without even reading what she has written. It becomes the teacher's and parent's job to help students understand what plagiarism is and what the consequences are for taking credit for work that is not their own. Many schools now require students to submit their papers to a plagiarism-screening Web site before turning them in.

"Drift." Another potential concern regarding Internet access at school is "drift": while on the Internet, your child is just a click away from intriguing nonacademic material such as her favorite band's Web site. If the teacher or librarian isn't monitoring vigorously, there's potential for plenty of wasted time.

? What should you look for in the use of computers at your child's school?

Take a tour of the media center and computer lab during your school's open house. Watching a demonstration of how computers are promoting your child's learning and paving his way into the workforce of the twenty-first century, you may well come away impressed and excited. But while you are at your child's school, ask some questions to make sure all this technology is being well used.

Evaluating School Computer Use:
Questions for Parents to Consider

- What is the school's acceptable use policy (AUP)? What are the consequences for failing to act responsibly when using online resources?

- Do the school and the district have a technology plan? Does the plan contain instructional objectives—goals for integrating computers with content being taught in the different subject areas?

- Can your child explain what the experience of working at the computer is adding to his learning and what the advantage is to using it?

- Does the school have a technology protection measure to manage Internet content and block access to known sites that contain questionable material for students?

- Are students supervised when using the Internet?

- What procedures are in place to make sure students are not doing too much "drifting" during working time?

- Where are the Internet-connected computers located? Who gets access to them?

- What kind of training does school staff have in the use of the Internet as a teaching tool? What kind of support is in place?

- Is the school aware of the physical health impact of sustained computer usage? Is the amount of screen time monitored? Are chairs and keyboards adjusted appropriately, and are there supports for using the keyboard and mouse?

Along with these questions, keep in mind some practices you *don't* want to see at your child's school, including over-reliance on computers for repetitive drill-and-practice exercises, time wasted by some students while others use the equipment, and computers used as a way to create quiet in the classroom.

How can technology and instruction be integrated?

Technology is more than a medium: it can be used in conjunction with the curriculum to provide learning opportunities that derive specifically from technology. Connected to an exciting world of current information, your child will develop insight while her teacher demonstrates how to navigate and reason through the labyrinth of sources available on the Internet in order to gather and interpret information.

What does this integrated educational experience look like? Let's say your child is in a foreign language or social studies class, working alone or in a group to research a travel destination, set up an itinerary, and create a journal of her experiences to share with her classmates. The teacher might begin by having students brainstorm what they think might be in a travel journal. Together the class will come up with important features such as names, dates, daily entries, personal comments, and some fun captions for photos. Then, once your child has selected the travel destination, she will spend a predetermined number of class periods doing research. She might start by using the Internet and find five specific sites to visit. The teacher will monitor and check this work. As your child takes notes, she will write down the complete Web site address for each fact she finds, along with Web addresses for any photos or other images she might want to include.

Your child will also draw on information from books in the classroom or the school library. When she starts compiling her journal, she will create her own text, adding it to the photos. Eventually she will complete a travel journal, and the teacher will provide time for her and her classmates to present their work to one another.

Through such a lesson, your child is learning how to use Internet sources, determining what is appropriate for the assignment, and also using other sources (books, magazines, music) to demonstrate understanding of another culture. At the same time, she is learning how to manage time effectively and deliver a project on time.

The presence of computers and software in the classroom alone cannot produce such results. Underlying this technology-enhanced learning environment is the foundation established by the school and the teacher, including:

- a curriculum integration specialist to formulate ways to create lessons utilizing technology

- lesson plans evolved from this basic concept that make use of the technology to deepen and enliven the learning process

- teachers trained in how to use the technology

- a technical support person available to deal with any problems

- up-to-date hardware and software that include computers, a high-speed Internet connection, multimedia software, resource compact discs (CDs) and DVDs in the relevant subject areas, a display or projection device, a scanner, a printer, and access to a computer lab where each student can work individually

If your child uses computers regularly in school, she is likely to want to use them outside of school, too. If you don't have a computer or Internet access at home, look for access in your local community. Many libraries, colleges, and cyber cafés offer equipment and free online connections for public use. Call your local library for more information.

How tech-savvy does your child need to be?

The reality is not all schools have a broad-based technology-enhanced curriculum. So what's the bottom line? What does your child need to know?

The essentials—the core skills of computer-based learning—are keyboarding (typing fluidly and using keyboard controls), conducting research on the Internet, and using the four basic operations of word processing, spreadsheets, database management, and graphics.

A broader measure comes from the International Society for Technology in Education (ISTE), which proposes these benchmarks for what students should be able to do:

By the end of second grade

- Use input devices (mouse, keyboard).
- Use output devices (monitor, printer).
- Work cooperatively in using technologies.

By the end of fifth grade

- Use telecommunications resources to engage in collaborative problem-solving tasks.

- Use technology tools for individual and collaborative writing and publishing activities.

By the end of eighth grade

- Collaborate with peers, experts, and others using telecommunications.

- Design, develop, and present products using technology resources.[5]

If you don't see progress toward these goals at your child's school, start by asking your child's teacher about the school's technology plan and standards. Carry your concerns and ideas to the curriculum coordinator, the principal, other parents, and the school board.

What is the purpose of the school's Web site?

Increasingly, schools have Web sites that can convey a range of information: school address and phone numbers, links to school staff, calendar of events, updates about school closings and other emergencies, curriculum information, and homework assignments in individual classrooms. The primary purpose of a school Web site is to communicate effectively with you, the parent community. A Webmaster or Internet director runs the site; the school principal is responsible for its content.

Schools can elect to have their Web site serve additional purposes related to their educational mission. These include, but are not limited to:

- online student newspaper publication

- yearbook

- student literary magazines

▥ teacher-created class information

▥ publication of appropriate student classwork

Your child's teacher may also maintain an instructional page on the school's site in order to post homework assignments and class information and offer links to instructional sites on other servers that have a purpose directly related to the educational mission of the school.

School districts, state Departments of Education, and the federal Department of Education also maintain their own Web sites. On your district's site, you are likely to find information about the entire school system and its programs, courses, testing, documents, and forms, as well as links to other educational resources.

Parents are seeing more and more data about school performance on their school district's Web site. The No Child Left Behind Act (NCLB) requires that each district give itself an annual report card based on results from federally mandated standardized tests. These scores must reflect results for different groups of students: students of varying races or ethnicities, low-income students, students with disabilities, and students with limited English-language skills. You should also see accurate and complete listings of teacher qualifications, dropout rates, and a report of whether your school has made adequate yearly progress (AYP) under NCLB. Information about each individual school must be included in the school district report card. You can also compare your child's school to others in the district and to others in your state. (For more detailed information on NCLB and testing, see Chapters 8 and 9.)

❓ What other uses of the Internet can you expect to see at your child's school?

Want to check up on your child's grades? Chances are you can do this via the Internet. Posting students' grades online has become increasingly popular around the country. Online programs, both commercial and school-created, give parents a better way to keep tabs on their children's progress. Some systems even provide you with your child's homework assignments, period-by-period attendance records, and discipline reports, in addition to his grades.

To protect family privacy, most programs require parents to have a password to access their child's records. Teachers will not routinely email the password when asked, given the lack of security surrounding email, but will either give the password to the student to deliver to his parents or will communicate the password in some other safe way. Most teachers appreciate the cyber system, because with online postings students can readily see what their grades are. Parents can, too, so everybody involved can always know the score!

Just like other members of the community, teachers have become increasingly dependent on email, using it to:

- Send electronic newsletters home to parents.
- Inform parents about any problems their child might be having at school or about any high points of the day.
- Reply to parent email inquiries.
- Submit lesson plans or reports to administrators.
- Chat with colleagues in the same school or elsewhere in the district.
- Share information about school events, programs, awards.

If you want to contact your child's teacher, email is most likely the best way to do it. For most teachers, checking and responding to email has become routine. And since teachers generally can't stop in the middle of the day—even during recess or lunch—to deal with phone calls, email makes it easy to communicate at everybody's convenience and to make an appointment for a phone call or an in-person meeting as necessary. This does not mean that all business should be conducted via email; it's best not to use email to discuss confidential information about your child, owing to the possibility of other people reading it.

Other uses of the Internet include the weekly email home that many elementary school teachers favor. This can include upcoming test dates, school meetings, what's going on in the classroom, and any highlights of the week that they want to share with parents. If you don't have access to the Internet, let the teacher know and make arrangements for another way to exchange information about your child and about the everyday doings of the class.

Where can you find out more?

Besides the resources listed here, check the American Library Association Web site (www.ala.org), which answers questions about the importance of the Internet for children and provides a guide to numerous great sites for kids (see page 18 for more information).

Children's Software Press
720 Kuhlman Road
Houston, TX 77024
713-467-8686
www.childsoftpress.com
A good resource for some basic information for you and your child, call or visit the Web site to order booklets including *The Incredible Internet: What Parents and Teachers Really Need to Know* by Merle Marsh, Ed.D., and *Writing a Paperless Paper: Student Guide to Electronic Study Skills* by James G. Lengel.

GetNetWise
1634 Eye Street NW, Suite 1107
Washington, DC 20006
202-638-4370
www.getnetwise.com
The GetNetWise site can help if you're worried about your child's Internet safety at home. You'll find a wizard to help you choose Internet safety tools that fit your needs. Simply check off a series of boxes detailing your specific requirements.

Learn the Net
9 Nebraska Street
San Francisco, CA 94110
415-826-2727
www.learnthenet.com
This is a great place for you to find a clear explanation of all things online, from Internet basics to joining newsgroups to privacy protection. With user-friendly language and helpful diagrams, this site is sure to help Internet users of all skill levels.

SuperKids
P.O. Box 4914
Mountain View, CA 94040
650-961-0321
www.superkids.com
This is a Web site for parents looking for sources of good educational software for their children. SuperKids provides reviews and ratings of educational software, practical tools for online and offline use, and news about important educational issues.

Chapter Notes

1. Market Data Retrieval, "The K–12 Technology Review 2005," 2005.

2. *Education Week*, Editorial Projects in Education Research Center, "The Information Edge," May 2006, pp. 54, 55.

3. Education Commission of the States, State Notes, "Technology, Cyber Schools," May 2004, p. 2.

4. *Education Week*, Editorial Projects in Education Research Center, "The Information Edge," May 2006, pp. 54, 55.

5. International Society for Technology in Education, National Educational Technology Standards for Students, "Profiles for Technology Literate Students," 2004.

UNDERSTANDING REPORTING SYSTEMS AND COMMUNICATION TOOLS

You want regular, clear information about how your child is doing in school. Report cards, grades and test scores, conferences, online communications, and phone calls are all tools the school and teacher use to stay in touch about your child's progress. Today's schools report not only on grades but also on each student's performance relative to state-specific standards. These reports have a big impact on you and your child. This chapter will demystify the purpose and meaning of report cards and grades and examine the variety of communication tools the school might employ to provide timely information about your child's academic progress, school activities, and social behavior. It also offers suggestions for helping if your child is struggling in school.

What is the purpose of grading?

For teaching and learning to be effective, teachers need to regularly check on how their students are doing. They need to find out who's learning well, who's not, and what particular problems students are experiencing. In addition to checking for understanding, teachers need to judge students' competence and evaluate the merits of student performance at a specific time. That's what grading is all about. Some of the purposes of grading include:

- to provide you with information about your child's progress in school

- to give this information to your child for use in self-evaluation

- to identify or group students for certain educational paths or programs

- to provide incentives for children to learn

- to evaluate the effectiveness of instructional programs

Grading involves the collection and evaluation of evidence of your child's achievements or performance. This process could include results from a single demonstration such as a quiz, an assignment, or an oral presentation, or from a number of assignments evaluated over an extended time. This time period is usually referred to as a grading period, and may be six weeks, nine weeks, a semester, or an entire year. At the end of each grading period, most public schools issue report cards. Elementary and middle schools also may require teachers to send home interim reports in the middle of the grading period for students who are having difficulty. These reports will probably include a grade, recommended strategies for improving performance, and information on contacting your child's teacher. There are also teachers who like to send interim reports on *every* student, so that parents have frequent updates on their children's progress. If you receive such a report, follow up by talking to your child about it and, if you have questions or concerns, get in touch with the teacher. Even if you don't receive an interim report on your child, you can always call or email the teacher to touch base.

❓ What's going on with report cards?

If you've compared current report cards with those from a few years ago, you know that they are in a state of evolution. A brief look at the history of report cards is informative: In the late 1800s, the first student report cards typically consisted of a list of basic skills and indicated which of these the student had mastered and which needed practice. By the middle of the 20th century, this list was being replaced by a number grade and then, eventually, by a letter grade (A, B, C), indicating a student's progress toward a specified standard. In the 1990s, educational leaders struggled to devise more effective ways of evaluating and reporting student progress. Often these efforts included lists of specific skills in a variety of subject areas and a reporting method that identified a student's progress through the skill levels. As issues of competition, comparison, and self-esteem were raised, some elementary schools began to replace the letter-grade report card with one featuring teacher comments and individualized assessment, using neutral descriptors such as *advanced, proficient,* and *basic.*

What About the Bell Curve?

One system of grading you are unlikely to see much of in your child's classroom anymore is the bell curve. Under this system, once widely used across the United States, the teacher created a test on which most students would score near the middle of a bell-shaped grading curve, while only a few would score low (on the left side of the curve) or high (on the right side of the curve). This type of grading curve is no longer the norm for teacher-made assessments in elementary and secondary public school classrooms. However, you can expect to see a bell curve in use on statewide standardized tests that are norm-referenced. (See Chapter 9 for more information on this type of testing.)

Today, report cards may feature skills lists, letter or number grades, and teacher narratives. And the advent of standards-based education has taken the evolution of report cards one step further: Districts are also required to report on each student's performance relative to state-specific standards. This means, for instance, that where a report card once noted performance simply in "Reading," standards now focus on specific reading benchmarks such as whether students have acquired an adequate knowledge of words for the grade level, can use a variety of strategies for understanding what they read, and can respond to literature. Performance related to the benchmarks is noted on the report card. As an example, under "Citizenship," your child could earn separate grades for "Demonstrates self-control," "Demonstrates respect," "Maintains positive attitude," "Follows class rules," "Follows school rules," and "Talks at appropriate times." Although private schools are not required to report on how students measure up to state standards, many of them have developed report cards that fulfill a similar function.

How can you make sense of your child's report card?

In creating a standards-based report card, most school districts have maintained a similar reporting format across grade levels, while also listing different standards on the reporting form for each grade level. Thus, the basic form of the report card is consistent from year to year, but the standards on the first-grade reporting form are different from those listed on the second-grade form, and so on. This gives parents a clear picture of the increasing complexity of the standards, academic and behavioral, at each subsequent grade level. The sample kindergarten and third-grade report cards on pages 108–109 illustrate how this kind of reporting works.

Variations on this approach abound. For example, a few years ago teachers in the Municipal School District in Cleveland, Ohio, simply provided a grade for each subject. Today, while the teachers still provide those grades, they also include course "outcome indicators" to give parents a sense of the progress their child is making in a particular area. Students are graded on a scale of 1 to 4, with the scale measuring how well students are meeting state standards. A grade of 1 means a student attempts the standard, while a 4 means a student exceeds the standard. As another example, in the Conejo Valley Unified School District in Thousand Oaks, California, progress on standards is measured on a scale of A (advanced) through F (failing—not meeting minimum criteria for promotion). Effort is evaluated separately on a scale of E (excellent) through U (unsatisfactory).

Kindergarten Progress Toward Standards

Rubric

4* = Exceeds trimester standards
4 = Meets trimester standards
3 = Making significant progress toward meeting trimester standards
2 = Making limited progress toward meeting trimester standards
1 = Does not meet trimester standards

☐ Same as overall mark
⊞ Relative strength to overall mark
◻I◻ Relative weakness to overall mark
☒ Not assessed at this time

ACADEMIC STANDARDS

MATHEMATICS

Number Sense	NOV	MAR	JUN
Counts to 100 by 1s		3	4
Counts to 100 by 5s			+
Counts to 100 by 10s	+	+	+
Recognizes numerals (0–30)	+	+	+
Prints numbers (0–30) correctly	+	+	+
Demonstrates 1-to-1 correspondence (1–30)		I	+
Uses concrete objects to add and subtract		I	+

Algebra & Functions	NOV	MAR	JUN
Identifies, sorts, and classifies objects by attribute			

Measurement & Geometry	NOV	MAR	JUN
Compares the length, width, height, and weight of objects	I		
Understands the concept of time as it applies to a day (e.g., morning, afternoon), a week, and a year			
Identifies and describes common geometric shapes and objects			

Statistics, Data, & Probability	NOV	MAR	JUN
Identifies, describes, and extends simple patterns			
Creates and records own patterns			+
Collects data and records results using objects, pictures, and graphs	I		

Mathematical Reasoning	NOV	MAR	JUN
Uses manipulatives and pictures to solve problems and to explain reasoning	I		

LANGUAGE ARTS

Reading

Reading	NOV	MAR	JUN
Follows words from left to right and top to bottom on printed page	3	3	4
Tracks words in a sentence	+	+	+
Recognizes that sentences include separate words and words include separate letters	+	+	+
Recognizes and names uppercase and lowercase letters of the alphabet	+	+	+
Matches consonant and short vowel sounds to appropriate letters		+	+
Identifies and produces rhyming words			
Reads simple 1-syllable and high frequency words			
Distinguishes fantasy from fact			
Connects information and events in text to life experiences			
Independently chooses reading activities	I	I	I

Writing

Writing	NOV	MAR	JUN
Prints name independently attending to form and spacing			
Prints uppercase and lowercase letters in sequence attending to form and spacing			

Spelling

Spelling	NOV	MAR	JUN
Phonetically spells words through guided activities	2	3	4
Spells independently using letter/sound knowledge			+

Listening & Speaking

Listening & Speaking	NOV	MAR	JUN
Listens actively and attentively	2	3	4
Speaks in complete sentences	+	+	+
Understands and follows 2-step and 3-step directions			
Describes people, places, and things			
Recites short poems, rhymes, and songs			
Retells a story in logical sequence	I		I

3rd Grade Progress Toward Standards

Rubric

4* = Exceeds trimester standards
4 = Meets trimester standards
3 = Making significant progress toward meeting trimester standards
2 = Making limited progress toward meeting trimester standards
1 = Does not meet trimester standards

☐ Same as overall mark
⊞ Relative strength to overall mark
⊟ Relative weakness to overall mark
☒ Not assessed at this time

ACADEMIC STANDARDS

MATHEMATICS

	NOV	MAR	JUN
MATHEMATICS	3	4	4
Number Sense			
Mastered (+) and (−) facts to 20	⊞	⊞	⊞
Counts, reads, and writes numbers to 10,000	⊞	⊞	⊞
Identifies place value of each digit to 10,000	⊞	⊞	⊞
Finds the sum of two whole numbers up to 5 digits			
Finds the difference between two whole numbers up to 5 digits			
Memorizes the multiplication tables through 10			
Solves multiplication problems using 4 digits by a single digit			
Divides 3-digit numbers evenly by a single digit			
Adds and subtracts simple fractions using picture cues			
Algebra & Functions			
Writes and solves simple equations			
Measurement & Geometry			
Chooses appropriate units and tools to measure			
Identifies and describes polygons			
Identifies, describes, and classifies common geometric objects			⊞
Statistics, Data, & Probability			
Conducts probability experiments and summarizes results			
Can read and interpret graphs			
Mathematical Reasoning			
Solves problems using a variety of strategies and explains reasoning			1

LANGUAGE ARTS

	NOV	MAR	JUN
Reading	2	3	4
Uses a variety of word attack skills to decode unfamiliar words	⊞		
Applies word analysis skills to vocabulary development			
Comprehends material at a literal level			
Comprehends material at a critical level			
Reads aloud fluently and accurately			1
Sustains independent reading regularly			
DIBELS results*	75	90	110
SRI results**	440	500	700
Writing	2	3	3
Writes complete sentences using a variety of formats	⊞		
Creates paragraphs with a topic sentence, supporting details and closing statement			
Uses revision strategies to improve writing			
Edits writing for mechanics and grammar			
Writes legibly			
Spelling	2	3	4
Spells correctly on spelling tests	⊞		
Spells correctly in writing			1
Speaking	3	4	4
Effectively presents in front of an audience	⊞		
Asks questions that clarify, responds to questions appropriately			

3rd Grade Reading Benchmarks

*DIBELS Scores = 110 words per minute
**SRI Scores = 500–800 lexile level

A standards-based system is criterion-referenced and does not report a comparison of your child's performance with that of others in the class. Instead, her performance is measured against clear statements of what she and others at the same grade level are expected to know and be able to do, based on a set body of content. In the past, report cards may have compared one student's performance to that of other students, but the only time you are likely to see this comparison now is along with your child's score on national and state standardized tests.

Regardless of what your child's report card looks like, you are likely to have questions about what it all means. Few of the markings are self-explanatory, although the card itself should contain a definition of terms. Many of the grading forms also contain space for written comments by the teacher. Here is where the teacher can give you more specific references to your child's everyday performance at school. These can cover everything from particular academic issues ("Excels at grasping the concept underlying math problems") to personal behavior ("Would be a better student if less distracted in class").

? What other reporting methods do schools use?

Report cards are the centerpiece of the school's reporting system. Their primary purpose is to communicate information to parents about teachers' assessments of students' achievement and performance in the classroom, to guide any necessary improvements, and to let parents know how their children are progressing in relation to state standards. Most schools employ a variety of other reporting tools to keep parents and students informed, including the following:

Standardized assessment reports. These give the results of the tests and assessments required by the state under No Child Left Behind (NCLB). The assessments are typically given once a year, and because they must be sent to the testing company to be scored, test results generally are not available until several months after students take the tests. Results are issued publicly on a statewide basis, as well as by district and school, but you should receive your child's individual scores by mail. Unlike a school report card, these reports give two types of scores:

1. the student's percentile rankings on the commercially pre-pared tests (often used for reading and math), showing where the child performed compared to a group of same-grade students, selected nationally, who have taken this exam before

2. the student's score on exams created by your state department of education or related agencies, indicating the child's success in mastering state standards

Online grading. Gaining popularity around the U.S., online grading allows you and your child immediate, up-to-date access to grades. Some systems also provide you with your child's homework assignments, period-by-period attendance, and discipline reports. To ensure privacy, students have individual passwords for viewing their grades only, not those of the entire class.

An extension of this idea is a computer software program for teachers that combines many functions including online grading, classroom reports, homework assignments, and notes to parents and students. These streamlined programs, designed to facilitate communication between teachers and parents, are currently being introduced in various school districts around the country and are likely to be in your child's future.

Parent-teacher conferences. A conference is an excellent way for teachers to report progress and for parents (and children) to discuss concerns and next steps. Communication at parent-teacher conferences is interactive and completely individualized to focus on your child. Since the teacher sees your child at both work and play, she or he can provide specific information about how your child is doing academically in all the subject areas, as well as developmentally and socially. And a conference presents a two-way opportunity for dialogue: parents can plan ahead, write down their questions, ask their child for suggestions, and be ready to be a full partner in the conversation.

Student-led conferences. Popular in many districts, these conferences give students the responsibility for leading the discussion and reporting on their learning to their parents. The teacher serves primarily as facilitator and observer.

Student-led conferences generally take place in the spring—an ideal time to get an overview of how the year has been going. Most teachers still favor a traditional parent-teacher conference in the fall, a time to set the stage for what's going well and what needs improving, while it's still fairly early in the school year. The kind of in-depth reporting involved in a student-led conference can only happen later on, partly because it requires quite a bit of preparation and collaboration between teacher and student.

Be aware that there may be issues that parents and teachers want to discuss without the student present, necessitating a separate meeting. Know, too, that because student-led meetings involve a great deal of extra work on the part of the teacher, not every teacher is enthusiastic about them.

Homework assignments. For most teachers, the purpose of homework is to offer students additional practice on what they learned in class in order to reinforce that learning. Other types of homework allow students to explore topics of special interest through reports and independent projects. Homework assignments also can help you to see what the teacher is emphasizing in class, what is expected of your child, and how your child is mastering the assigned work.

Personal communication. There was a time when a phone call was the easiest and most efficient means of getting information, but in the era of email, the phone tends to be used less frequently. As a parent, you may fear phone calls, since it seems that the only reason the teacher calls is to announce bad news about your child. Teachers, too, often lament that the only time they hear from parents is when there is a complaint to be made. To change this pattern, many schools have initiated programs in which teachers make regular phone calls to parents just to chat, with no set agenda.

Teachers have traditionally written letters to notify parents when their child has done excellent work or, alternatively, if an academic or social problem has arisen. In similar fashion, parents' letters to teachers may inform them of an important event taking place in their child's life, such as a divorce or the death of a pet. Both teachers and parents have discovered that the post office is generally more reliable than a child's backpack!

Email is used more and more for effective parent-teacher communication. At the beginning of the year, your child's teacher will most likely ask for your email address, if you have one. Most school Web pages include a listing of the email address of all administrators, teachers, and other staff members. If you have a concern or question about your child, you can email the teacher without worrying that you are interrupting her busy schedule. You should expect a response within twenty-four hours; if you don't receive one, try the phone.

? What's a good way to discuss grades and report cards with your child?

Perhaps you're one of those parents who consciously or unconsciously avoids discussions about grades with your child because it brings back bad memories of your own school experiences. Maybe you recall your disappointment and anger at getting that really low grade for the science project that you'd spent the whole weekend on, while the class "star" got an A for something that took a couple of hours. Or you might be afraid of putting too much emphasis on grades because you remember the academic pressure you felt from your parents and don't want to subject your child to the same thing.

Teachers sometimes face this situation. One teacher remembers being confused when she found a student in tears over the A– she had just earned on a project. The girl's parents had told her that anything less than an A was unacceptable, so the child was afraid to take the less-than-completely-perfect project home.

Whatever the reason for discomfort in discussing the importance of good grades, when parents don't discuss them, children may get the message that grades don't matter as long as learning is taking place. The problem with this approach is that a child may decide not to do the work anymore if it's the learning that counts, not the grade. He can argue that, after all, he is learning something. Likewise, not all students are convinced by the argument that they need good grades in order to move on and eventually graduate.

Whether ambivalent about grades or very focused on them, parents sometimes view grades as labels (for example, a C on the report card may mean that they view their child as a "C student"). When parents take this view—or when children believe that they do—children often avoid discussions of their work in school, especially when they're experiencing problems. Not wanting to disappoint or anger their parents, they steer clear of grade discussions, screen the phone calls at home, and try to get to the mailbox first when a grade report is due.

A more effective strategy is to take a balanced approach to the importance of grades. Let your child know that grades are important and that high grades will require his best effort. At the same time, help your child see that a grade is a short-term measuring tool, not a permanent one. Grades relate to a particular set of tasks performed at a particular time, and things can change. Low grades can be improved with additional work and, by the same token, high grades might drop if the quality of the work falls off.

In discussing grades with your child, be sure to talk about the teacher's grading practices. Your child should be familiar with them, and so he should find such discussions relevant. With the advent of online grading programs, now in common use, teachers have to be accountable for grades in a very exact way. With a middle school English class, for example, it will be easy for you to see what proportions of the grades are devoted to in-class work, homework, quizzes, tests, projects, and so forth. Stress to your child that the primary purpose of grades is *not* to label him ("problem student," "A student," "average student") but rather to let you both know how he is doing in school and where he might need additional help. Understanding this, he is likely to be more willing to discuss his schoolwork with you.

Consider, too, talking about grades and reporting at other times—not just when report cards are due. Include grades as part of the regular conversations you have with your child about school.

Doing well in school requires that children understand what is expected of them. Most teachers do a good job of communicating this, but if your child is baffled or discouraged by a low grade, encourage him to talk to his teacher. If expectations were unclear, he should ask the teacher to explain what was expected in the assignment and then find out what steps he can take to improve performance in the future. If the teacher is unaware that your child is really struggling in a particular area, then your child needs to let the teacher know that, too. A caveat: Some ways to approach a teacher with a question about grading are going to be more graciously received than others. As one science teacher from Camarillo, California, puts it, "Having a student ask me where he fell short or how he can improve next time is very different from having him tell me I've made a mistake in grading his paper."

Of course, it may be that the teacher really *has* made a mistake. Teachers are human, after all. If you believe this is the case, have your child first tell the teacher that he doesn't understand why he received this grade. Most teachers will have no problem admitting to an honest mistake and correcting the grade. However, if the teacher disagrees and the explanation doesn't convince your child, ask to meet with the teacher yourself. The school principal is your last recourse if you are still concerned that a grade is inaccurate or unfair.

Children seek the approval of their parents, and if you let your child know that his academic accomplishments are valued, he will be encouraged to do well in the future. Celebrating a good report card with a trip to a movie or a special "certificate" on the refrigerator is a great way to do this, but for most children it's enough to hear Dad's or Mom's praise and open expression of pride. (Stay away from major monetary rewards, though, or your child will learn to put more value on the reward than on the learning, and you may soon be out-of-pocket.) More important, help your child develop his own personal pride in an improved grade or an especially good report card. Let your comments and questions encourage his internal sense of accomplishment: "You must be really proud." "How do you feel about this?" "Wow, how did you do that?"

Making the Grade

A mother in Santa Monica, California, saw that her 11-year-old son's writing kept improving through the semester, and so she could not understand why his report card showed that his grade had gone down. "He professed total ignorance of what was going on and declared that the teacher must have it in for him, so I decided to talk to her," Mom explained. "I found out that my son had been working well recently, but he had neglected to tell me that he hadn't completed any assignments for the first two months of the semester."

Even the sharpest and most well-intentioned child can sometimes get low grades, and how you respond to these can make a big difference. Punishing your child for poor grades is likely to result in his choosing not to discuss schoolwork with you in the future. Rather, talk together about the grade; try to determine if it's a one-time slip or a signal that additional work is needed. In the latter case, you may need to impose certain restrictions. Be prepared to enforce them. If your child needs to put in more time on homework and needs a quiet place to study, you may have to adjust your schedule to accommodate him. Doing so will show your child that you regard learning and schoolwork as important. And if further help is needed, check with his teacher about the best way to secure it.

How important *are* report cards and grades?

Your child should have a clear idea of the importance the teacher places on grades and what importance you place on them. Although it is hard to know exactly how your child will do in a grading period, it's not a good sign if her grade constantly catches you by surprise. If this happens, you know you need to be in closer touch with how and what your child is doing at school. Also be aware that under the regulations governing most school systems, a student cannot earn a failing grade on a report card without her parents receiving some prior warning. The idea is to give the student and parent time to turn things around. It's also possible that there has been a mistake and the grade is inaccurate.

Report cards and grades do count, and there can be consequences for what the report card says about your child's performance. Schools often use some form of ability grouping, and your child's grades can play a role in what teachers your child is assigned to, which students she works alongside, and the level at which she's expected to perform.

In the big picture, however, it is only in high school that your child's grades start to "count" in the sense that colleges or future employers will want to see them. The exception to this, happening more frequently nowadays, is if your youngster takes a high school course while still in middle school. In that case, those course grades may count, too.

An additional note: Almost all report cards list the number of days absent and tardy. Pay attention to this number, because it helps you monitor your child's attendance. You want to make sure that the school's record matches your own.

What can you do if your child is struggling academically?

At some point in his school career, it's likely that your child will face bumps in the road. Having experienced this both as a parent and a teacher, I can assure you that although this may feel like the end of the world for both of you, it isn't. You may be in for long hours of helping your child, but you won't be the first parent to do this! Children are all different, not all of them fit the set academic mold, and schools are equipped to deal with this. Helping a student who is having difficulty is one of the most rewarding aspects of a teacher's job.

Low grades may be the first indication that your child needs help, but there are other possible indicators. You have reason to be concerned if your child:

- has grades that are slipping dramatically or creeping down from grading period to grading period
- expresses intense dislike of school
- takes an excessive amount of time to complete homework
- is significantly behind his peers academically
- works hard, yet never seems to catch up
- has not been helped by prior efforts to improve his schoolwork
- has sinking self-esteem in relation to his studies

It's natural for children to be excited about learning and to want to do well, so if this is not happening with your child, something is amiss. You will need to play detective to figure out what. Talking to him directly is the best place to start, but you may find that he doesn't want to talk about it or that he grows defensive or even hostile when you try to question him.

If this happens, set up a conference with the teacher. Since success is the leading motivator in school achievement, you ideally want to address the problem before your child begins to experience significant failure. Here are some pointers for that first meeting:

- Make it clear that you have concerns about your child's academic work and that you don't want him to fall behind.

- Ask for specific information in all areas: academics and work habits, social skills such as interaction with other students, and behavior in the classroom. Ask about everything the teacher notices including your child's self-confidence, sense of responsibility, and happiness.

- Express your desire to work with the teacher to solve your child's academic problems. Explain that you are prepared to do all you can at home to support your child's learning. Discuss how the school can help, how you can help, and what extra help, such as tutoring, might be needed. Many parents and teachers believe that one-on-one tutoring is the most effective means of intervening on behalf of a struggling child. Some schools have staff who can tutor students or offer peer tutoring, which can prove very helpful. Don't hesitate to ask about low-cost programs or possible financial help for tutoring.

- Request periodic updates from the teacher. Explain that you don't want to wait until the next report card to find out how your child is doing.

If it takes a while to get to the root of your child's struggles, don't give up. Find the cause and you will usually find a solution. Basically, you want to learn whether the problem is related to missing knowledge, skills, or foundational concepts; to lack of motivation; or to emotional stress that can be addressed in the classroom. Having identified the cause, you can work with your child, the teacher, and others at the school to help turn the situation around.

Schools have processes in place to intervene and work with struggling students. In addition, federal law directs schools to work with *all* struggling learners early and regularly in an effort to keep them from falling behind. From these directives, a formal process known as Response to Intervention (RTI) has emerged. RTI is intended to help schools provide high-quality interventions and continually monitor students' progress. Not all schools have begun to implement RTI approaches, but if your school has, this can be another resource for you in supporting your child.

Finally, if efforts you and the teacher make are unsuccessful, your child may have learning or medical difficulties that require more involved long-term solutions. (See Chapters 10 and 11 for more information on learning disabilities, behavioral disorders, and special education services.)

What if the teacher wants your child to repeat a grade?

Understandably, you are likely to be upset if you receive a retention recommendation for your child. Teachers give many reasons for recommending that a child be retained. Find out which one applies to you:

- Your child's scores on statewide or districtwide tests are well below grade level.
- Your child appears to be immature for her age.
- Your child has failed to reach performance levels expected for promotion to the next grade.

In many schools today, tests are being used to determine whether a student will go on to the next grade or repeat the same grade. More and more children are facing the possibility of retention because they're not achieving the test scores required to move up to the next grade. This may seem like a sound practice—a way to reduce social promotion, where a child automatically passes on to the next grade at the end of the school year regardless of whether she has mastered the skills and content she needs to know. However, if the approach to instruction isn't modified in some way, your child isn't likely to have greater success the second time around.

With this in mind, the National Association of School Psychologists (NASP) supports the position that both grade retention and social promotion are ineffective. Instead, NASP advocates what it calls "promotion plus"—specific interventions to ensure readiness for the next grade. Here are questions to consider for promotion plus:

- Could your child benefit from one-on-one tutoring in her areas of difficulty?
- Are options such as summer school, extended day, or extended year available?
- Is your child receiving extra support, such as small group work, to help her understand new ideas?
- What type of curriculum materials and instructional strategies does the teacher use? Could your child benefit from varied

instruction methods? For example, if she is a kinesthetic learner, meaning that she learns best by acting out situations, is she getting the opportunity to do this as she learns to read?

- Does your child resist your help with schoolwork? If so, is the school able to offer support?

- Have you worked with the teacher to identify ways to increase your child's success in the classroom?

- Would extracurricular activities such as soccer, dance, or karate help your child release some stress, gain self-confidence, and become motivated to do better in school?

Before agreeing to have your child retained for a year, the NASP advises that you consider your response to these questions and ask your child what she thinks would help. Talk to your child's teacher to see if she or he feels that implementing these interventions would provide the necessary support and make a difference in regard to the school's recommendation of retention.

How promotion or retention is determined varies from state to state, so you may or may not have to comply with the school's decision not to promote your child. Find out what your state law says about decision-making authority regarding retention, and follow up by asking your child's principal what the school district's policy is. (If your child is receiving special education services, make sure the IEP team is involved in the decision-making process.) Grade retention is a very difficult and emotionally charged decision; do all you can to work cooperatively with the school to reach an agreement. If the school still supports retention and you want another alternative, talk to your principal about state law and district policy to discover who makes the final decision and what the appeal process is.

Know, too, that although recent research has documented that outcomes for students who are retained generally are not positive,[1] the research on retention at all age levels is based on *group* data. There are many stories of *individual* students who have benefited from retention. Whatever is decided, plan on staying close to your child's academic and behavioral performance during the upcoming year, and work with her teachers to ensure that she is getting all the support she needs.

If your child is going to repeat a grade, experts suggest the following:

- Meet with the teacher to find out specifically what your child's achievements are and how best to help her in the upcoming year.

- Work through your own feelings, which may include disappointment, frustration, anger, sadness, or guilt.

- Talk to other adults, including parents with the same experience, to help you express your feelings and consider different opinions.

- Talk with your child. Plan a time and place where you can have a calm, uninterrupted conversation.

- Accept responsibility. When appropriate, you can explain to your child that she was placed in the wrong grade early, a grown-up's mistake.

- Recognize that you are the lightning rod; whatever attitude you express, your child will pick up on it.

What can you do if you believe your child is underachieving?

Underachieving students generally possess the academic ability to be in the top third of a class, but their actual achievement falls far short of that. This syndrome receives a lot of attention in most schools, since these youngsters, whose reasons for underachieving come in all shapes and sizes, present a real challenge.

Because underachieving may be due to a variety of reasons, there is no single way to solve the problem. You will need to try to figure it out, by first talking to your child to find out why he is not doing well. If you believe he may have a learning disability, consult the teacher, who may suggest a referral for further evaluation. If you have ruled out this possibility, there are several other possible causes for lack of motivation:

Academic burnout. In this age of high achievement and myriad extracurricular activities, your child may have just had it.

Emotional or social problems. If there are problems at home (for example, divorce or chronic illness), social studies class may seem mighty unimportant to your child. Depression, fears, anxiety, or stress can also be a factor in underachievement.

Boredom. It's easy for your child to say, "Yes, I'm bored, that's the reason." This may sound like a copout—and it may be one—but it's still a possibility. If your child complains of boredom, discuss it with the teacher.

Peer pressure. Your child's friends may not admire academic achievement. Since peer acceptance is important, help your child find a way to combine it with doing well at school.

Fear of failure. Your child may be so afraid of taking a risk, such as raising his hand or speaking up in class, that he falls behind.

A particular teacher. If your child has always done well in the past but is unable to keep up this year or has lost the desire to try, check out the teacher and what's going on in the classroom.

Your subsequent course of action will depend on what you have been able to sleuth out about your child. Whatever the solution, you will want to avoid getting into a push-pull situation. Sometimes, if you're having trouble getting things done that need to be done, setting or negotiating rules, rewards, and consequences can help get a child back on track. Of course, this depends on the child and the underlying cause. Structuring your home life so that education has a high priority is also important. Remember, too, that there's more to school than grades. As parents, we all may want our children to be high performers, but obviously not every child is capable of that, and those who are may not excel all the time. Avoid getting too hung up on grades. Instead, stress *learning.*

A brief word of caution: Some children, particularly in the early grades, may just not be developmentally ready for the challenges of the learning environment. It's always possible that your child is a late bloomer. Be open to that possibility, and remember that your child, like every human being, is a work-in-progress.

As my mother used to remind me, life is a journey, not a race. With all the headlines about high-stakes tests and the importance of standardized test scores, it's easy to forget that *how* your child moves forward is as vital as *where* he ends up. As with the rest of his growth, your child's educational journey probably will be an unsteady one, with some ebb and flow in grades—some days, weeks, and years where things go more smoothly than others. Your youngster has only one chance to be a child. With your help, he can make the most of it.

Where can you find out more?

Finding Help When Your Child Is Struggling in School by Lawrence J. Greene (New York: Golden Books, 1998) shows parents how to work within the educational system and how to go outside it when appropriate.

How's My Kid Doing? A Parent's Guide to Grades, Marks, and Report Cards by Thomas R. Guskey (San Francisco: Jossey-Bass, 2003). Down-to-earth information and advice help you make sense of school reports and build open communication with the teacher.

The Hurried Child: Growing Up Too Fast Too Soon, 25th Anniversary Edition by David Elkind (New York: Da Capo Lifelong Books, 2006). This fully updated classic provides insight, advice, and hope for encouraging healthy development while protecting the joy and freedom of childhood.

I Know My Child Can Do Better! A Frustrated Parent's Guide to Educational Options by Anne Rambo (New York: Contemporary Books, 2002) helps readers sort out the types of problems their children are having and offers a range of practical solutions.

Motivated Minds: Raising Children to Love Learning by Deborah Stipek and Kathy Seal (New York: H. Holt and Co., 2001) offers a practical guide to ensuring your child's success in school.

National Association of School Psychologists (NASP)
4340 East-West Highway, Suite 402
Bethesda, MD 20814
866-331-6277
www.nasponline.org
NASP offers an excellent guide to school retention: "Position Statement on Student Grade Retention and Social Promotion." The paper gives a good overview of the topic and presents alternative solutions.

Overcoming Underachieving: A Simple Plan to Boost Your Kids' Grades and End the Homework Hassles by Ruth Peters (New York: Broadway Books, 2000) offers some basic tips on working with your underachieving child.

Parenting a Struggling Reader by Susan L. Hall and Louisa C. Moats (New York: Broadway Books, 2002) is an excellent, step-by-step guide for parents, with plenty of first-hand accounts from parents who have been in this difficult situation.

"A Parent's Guide to Response-to-Intervention" (National Center for Learning Disabilities, 2006) is an informative parent-advocacy brief about RTI. To download it, go to www.ncld.org and choose "Parent Center" to find links to the guide and to other useful publications.

School Power: Study Skill Strategies for Succeeding in School by Jeanne Shay Schumm. (Minneapolis: Free Spirit Publishing, 2001). Written for kids ages 11 and up, this book presents practical advice on every conceivable topic including test preparation.

See Johnny Read! The 5 Most Effective Ways to End Your Son's Reading Problems by Tracey Wood (New York: McGraw-Hill, 2004) contains solid information on recognizing reading problems, finding tutoring, getting help from the school, and more.

True or False? Tests Stink! by Trevor Romain and Elizabeth Verdick (Minneapolis: Free Spirit Publishing, 1999) takes a humorous approach to helping kids ages 8–13 prepare and then do their best on test days.

What Happened to Recess and Why Are Our Children Struggling in Kindergarten? by Susan Ohanian (New York: McGraw-Hill, 2002). Ohanian believes that even children who are able test takers are hurt by the politics surrounding testing. She discusses why a child's success or failure is currently determined by a set of tests and what parents are doing to change public policy on education.

Chapter Notes

1. *School Psychology Review,* "Meta-Analysis of Grade Retention Research: Implications for Practice in the 21st Century" by S.R. Jimerson, 2001, vol. 30, no. 3, pp. 420–37, and American Educational Research Association, Educational Evaluation and Policy Analysis, "Effects of Kindergarten Retention Policy on Children's Cognitive Growth in Reading and Mathematics," 2005.

CHAPTER

8

THE NO CHILD LEFT BEHIND ACT

The notion of education laws may seem remote, yet knowing what the key laws are and how they might affect you can help you make a positive difference regarding the quality of the education your child receives. Although federal money accounts for only about 8 percent of spending on education, the passage of the No Child Left Behind Act in January 2002 marked the first time that the federal government had involved itself so fully in the administration of public education. The main focus of this legislation is to improve the academic achievement of every student regardless of ethnicity or economic status. The goal is to enable all students to perform at a proficient level, as defined by each state, by the 2013–14 school year.

What is No Child Left Behind?
How does it affect your child?

The No Child Left Behind Act (NCLB) is the most recent reauthorization of the federal government's biggest K–12 program, the Elementary and Secondary Education Act (ESEA), which began in 1965. Although NCLB is a federal program, each individual state must develop and implement its own academic standards, tests for measuring their achievement, and regulations for administering the program based on guidelines from the United States Department of Education. The most important points of NCLB include the following:

Standards. States must define and adopt challenging standards for what every child should know and be able to do. The standards are public documents you can get from your school, school district, or state Department of Education. They help you know what your child is expected to learn in school.

Testing. Beginning no later than the 2005–06 school year, all children must be tested in reading and math each year in grades 3–8, and once more in grades 10–12. Beginning in the 2007–08 school year, schools are also required to administer annual tests in science achievement at least once in grades 3–5, 6–9, and 10–12. All students in the same grade level throughout the state take the same test once a year. Tests are selected at the state level; states must adopt high-quality assessments that are aligned with their academic standards. This ensures that your child is tested on what the standards indicate she should know.

Public reporting. For the first time, states, districts, and schools across the United States must publicly report data to demonstrate how all students are progressing toward meeting these standards. "All students" means that the reported information must be broken down according to racial and ethnic group, gender, English language proficiency, migrant status, disability status, and low-income status. Schools must also report two-year trends in student achievement to see if the school is making progress, and they must provide information documenting the qualifications of their teachers.

Adequate yearly progress (AYP). The idea behind AYP is to hold the public education system accountable for teaching *all* students. States must set clear timelines for improving student achievement, with particular emphasis on closing achievement gaps between low-income and minority students and their peers. To do this, states must publish an AYP formula that details how they will determine the level of progress schools need to make each year, leading up to 2014. Each state sets a starting point based on the performance of its lowest-achieving student subgroup or its lowest-achieving schools, whichever is higher. The state then sets the level of student achievement that a school must attain after two years in order to continue to show AYP. Subsequent thresholds must be raised at least once every three years until, by 2014, all students in the state are achieving at the "proficient" level on state assessments in reading/language arts and math.

School improvement. A school is designated as needing improvement when, for two years in a row, state assessment data reveals that one or more groups of students are not making enough progress toward meeting standards. The state, school district, and school must then collaborate on a two-year plan that spells out precisely what each will do to improve student achievement. This school-improvement plan should also include what role parents and members of the broader community will play in implementing the plan. Further action must be taken if the school continues to be assessed as needing improvement in subsequent years.

Rights and responsibilities of parents. Under NCLB, you have a right to see your school, district, and state data on academic achievement, graduation rates, and the qualification of your child's teachers. Your school district is required to publish an annual student performance report card with information about performance at the school district and individual school levels. If your child is a public school student, you cannot legally refuse to allow her to be tested, unless she is exempted for a confirmed disability. For example, if your child has an IEP or 504 plan* that details specific testing conditions (such as being given extra

---

*This reference is to specialized individual education plans covered under laws for students with disabilities. See Chapter 11 for more information about special education.

time or having the test read aloud), then under NCLB she is still entitled to these provisions. And for children with severe cognitive disabilities, NCLB has authorized alternative assessments to measure whether AYP is being made. NCLB requires parents to be actively involved in the decision-making process at their school. Further, if your child attends a Title I school* that is designated in need of improvement, parents and community representatives must be part of a school team to help develop a plan of action to improve the school.

What are the academic standards your child must meet?

Standards are set at the state level. Some experts have advocated for national academic standards, but for now state standards are firmly in place as the foundation of NCLB, and this is unlikely to change in the immediate future. There are three types of standards:

1. **Academic standards** are statements about what all students should know and be able to do in the core academic subjects at each grade level.

2. **Content standards** describe basic agreement about the *body* of academic knowledge that all students should possess.

3. **Performance standards** describe what level of performance is sufficient for students to be rated at various proficiency levels, for example, *advanced, proficient, basic,* and *below basic.*

With standards in place, NCLB anticipates that excellent tests, solid teacher training, and revised curricula for learning will follow, so that all students receive the tools they need to meet increasingly higher academic expectations as they progress through the grades. When standards are well thought out, they build on the principle that young people develop their understanding of particular subjects over time as they acquire more sophisticated ways of thinking. The standards for each grade level and content area incorporate what teachers are required to teach

---

*A Title I school is one that receives special federal funding for economically disadvantaged students.

as well as the *learner outcomes* (what the student will be able to do) and guidelines for the specific thinking skills and problem-solving techniques required to achieve those outcomes.

Examples of Academic Standards

Third Grade

Number sense: Students understand the relationship between whole numbers, simple fractions, and decimals.

Reading: Students read and understand grade-level appropriate material. They draw upon a variety of comprehension strategies as needed.

Fifth Grade

Reading comprehension: Using grade-level appropriate material, students describe and connect the essential ideas, arguments, and perspectives of the text through use of their knowledge of text structure, organization, and purpose.

Word analysis: Students use their knowledge of word origins and word relationships, as well as historical and literary context clues, to determine the meaning of specialized vocabulary.

While states set academic, content, and performance standards for all subject areas, NCLB calls for proficiency in reading, math, and science. As with all other aspects of NCLB, implementation happens at the state level. This means that the picture around the country is quite varied. Standards are a work in progress, continually being reviewed and revised in order to keep them challenging for all students.

We need standards for excellence, fairness, and equity—to ensure that both curricula and assignments are challenging and grade-level appropriate. Standards indicate what your child is supposed to be learning. If he falls behind, knowing the standards can help both you and his teacher recognize his difficulty and respond before too much time passes. Even though teaching styles and methods will vary, standards ensure that the educational goals remain constant. Thus, knowing the standards will not only tell you what your child is supposed to learn but also assure him the opportunity to learn it.

Obtain a copy of your state's academic standards from your school or district office or from the Web site of your state Department of Education. Since education jargon can be confusing, it's a good idea to get together with other parents (and teachers if possible) to read them. Review them carefully, and don't hesitate to ask for clarification from your school.

After learning what standards your child must meet, take a look at his homework and classwork to see how they are aligned to the standards. Ask the teacher, "What are the children supposed to be learning through this assignment?" or "How does this assignment relate to the standards for fourth grade?" Not every piece of homework has to relate directly to a standard; nevertheless, asking questions is a good way to understand at a deeper level what your child's education is all about.

What reporting data are you entitled to, and how can you use it?

1. You have the right to receive an individual report of your child's performance on the state's academic achievement tests in a language and format that is easily understandable. The results will indicate which standards your child has and has not met, and it will provide clear information about any needs that may have been identified for her. You can then work with your child's teachers to address those needs.

2. Every school district that receives Title I funds (around 70 percent of school districts nationally) must issue a report card for each school in the district. These school reports must detail overall levels of student achievement as well as achievement levels broken down by subgroups of race, ethnicity, gender, English language proficiency, migrant status, disability status, and low-income status. Your school's report must also show student achievement levels compared to the district and the state by subject and student group. Other mandatory information includes two-year trends in student achievement at your child's school, whether your school has been labeled "in need of improvement," and information documenting the qualifications of your child's teachers.

3. Finally, your district and your state must issue reports providing the same information as the school report card for both the district and the whole state.

Armed with this data, you can compare your child's achievement levels to those of other children in your school, district, and state, and you can also compare the achievement levels of your child's school to comparable schools in your district and state. Drawing on this information, you can make informed choices about where to send your child to school. (For more on school choice, see Chapter 2.)

You also have a right to know about the status of your child's teacher—whether the teacher has emergency or temporary credentials and certification in the subject areas she or he teaches. While NCLB leaves it up to each state to set the criteria for what makes a teacher highly qualified, it does set as a baseline that highly qualified teachers must at least possess state certification and a bachelor's degree. Teachers of core academic subjects—math, language arts, science, social studies, foreign languages, and civics and government—must also demonstrate content-area expertise. If your child is in a Title I school and a teacher who is not highly qualified has taught your child for more than four weeks in a row, you must be notified in writing.

One of NCLB's initial goals was to guarantee every child be taught by a highly qualified teacher by the end of the 2005–06 school year. As states continued to formulate and tighten definitions for what this means, some teachers who were fully credentialed in the past were finding that their original qualifications did not measure up under the new rules. Because of this, the deadline was pushed back. This is why you may receive a report that your child's teacher has become underqualified. If you are concerned that your child's teacher is not well qualified, don't hesitate to make an appointment with the principal to discuss the matter.

What does it mean if your child's school is labeled "in need of improvement"?

To ensure that all students achieve the state's academic standards, NCLB requires states to establish stringent annual improvements for each school. This measurement is called adequate yearly progress (AYP). If a school's actual achievement is at or above the state goal in a given year, the school is designated as making AYP. If achievement is below the goal for two consecutive years, the school is designated as "in need of improvement."

If your child's school receives this label, your first step is to find out why. Each state has its own requirements to determine proficiency, and these requirements can vary considerably from state to state. For example, it could be that your school has not met the percentage-passing rate for the math section of the state test. Or, even if your school has met these goals, it may have fallen short in a particular subgroup, such as students with learning disabilities. Check your school's Web site or call the main office for details. Under NCLB, you have a right to know the specific areas in which the school needs to improve; what steps the state, district, and school will take to improve student achievement; and how you or other parents can be involved in the school improvement plan.

In addition, check to see if your child's school is a Title I school. This is important, because while all public schools in the U.S. receive an AYP rating, only Title I schools are required to *apply* the sanctions imposed when AYP is not met. If your child is in elementary school, chances are good that this applies to his school, since around 67 percent of individual public elementary schools in the U.S. receive Title I funds.

If your child attends a Title I school that has missed AYP goals for two years in a row, the school must offer him the opportunity to transfer to a different school within the district. If no alternative school is available, your child's current school must make an effort to enter into a cooperative agreement with another district to allow your child to transfer there. If this is the third year that your child's school is in need of improvement, then you are entitled to transfer *and* to receive supplemental services such as tutoring for your child. Four consecutive years of needing improvement means your school will face significant changes in leadership and curriculum, along with professional development for staff or other strategies. After five years on the list, the state can take over the school board, reconstitute the district, set up charter schools, or even privatize education. Finally, in year six, your local school district must reopen the school as a public charter school, replace all or most of the school staff, and turn school operations over to the state.

If your child attends a Title I school identified as needing improvement, the district is required to inform you about your options. For some parents, dealing with this in person makes more sense: go directly to the district office and find out exactly what options you have. If, for example, your child is eligible for a transfer, you will be applying through the district and not through the school. District officials are required to tell you what other schools in your district are available.

What are supplemental educational services? How can your child receive them?

Supplemental educational services are additional academic instruction available to students in schools that have not met state targets for increasing student achievement (meeting AYP) for three or more years. With supplemental services, your child can receive free after-school or weekend tutoring; the services are federally funded. If your child is eligible for supplemental services, your school or district is required to inform you by sending a notice, written in straightforward language, that lists all the accredited tutoring services near where you live. The services on this list have to be approved by the state, and the information should include a description of each one.

Most important, these services are free for your child, and the school district is required to make the arrangements for her to receive them. Once you have chosen a tutoring program, the district should negotiate a contract that specifies the number of sessions of instruction for your child, the length of each session, your child's learning goals, and a timetable for reaching those goals. You should get a copy of this information. Once your child begins tutoring, the program must work closely with your school and with you to make sure that it is helping your child with the specific difficulties she is having in school.

Choosing Supplemental Services: Questions to Ask

- How long has this tutoring service been in business?
- What is its record of success?
- Where are the services provided? Does my child need a computer and Internet access?

- If necessary, is transportation provided? (Districts are not required to provide this for supplemental services.)

- How are the services linked to the school curriculum?

- What does the service provider do to coordinate with my child's teachers?

- What is the student-to-tutor ratio? Obviously, one-to-one tutoring is best, but there should never be more than three students per tutor.

- What kinds of materials will the tutor send home so I can continue to work with my child at home?

- How often will the tutor report my child's progress to me and to her teacher at school? How will the reporting take place? By phone? In writing? In person?

Choosing a tutor is not easy. Be sure to talk to your child's teacher about what kind of help your child needs and which providers make the best sense for her.

NCLB has its passionate advocates and its detractors. However, all agree that its goals are laudable:

- closing the student achievement gap
- making public schools accountable
- setting standards of excellence for every child
- putting a qualified teacher in every classroom

As a parent, it's important that you understand your role in helping achieve these goals. To do this, stay informed, communicate regularly with teachers and other parents, and be willing and ready to exercise your rights in your child's best interest. In a May 2006 memo, U.S. Secretary of Education Margaret Spellings reported that only about 1 percent of parents of students eligible to transfer out of a low-performing school had exercised their child's right to do so. In addition to this, only about 17 percent of parents nationally are taking advantage of the supplemental educational services their children are entitled to.

Where can you find out more?

Pages 18–20 include a variety of resources to aid in your efforts to learn more about improving your child's school and school achievement, including the Center for Parent Leadership (CPL) and the National Education Association (NEA). Pages 38–40 highlight organizations and Web sites with information on choosing schools. Here are additional resources to help you understand No Child Left Behind:

Public Education Network (PEN)
601 13th Street NW, Suite 710
Washington, DC 20005
202-628-7460
www.publiceducation.org
PEN works to build public demand and mobilize resources for quality public education for all children. It offers detailed information about NCLB.

U.S. Department of Education
400 Maryland Avenue SW
Washington, DC 20202
800-872-5327
www.ed.gov/nclb
The U.S. Department of Education Web site has a section dedicated entirely to NCLB, containing detailed information for parents on the specifics of the law.

CHAPTER

9

EXAMINING STANDARDIZED TESTING

Testing is an especially significant topic these days. While quizzes and exams that teachers routinely use to check on students' learning are still the most common tests that your child encounters, standardized testing is the tool state and national agencies use to measure student performance. All sorts of pivotal decisions hinge on how children perform on standardized tests. This chapter will answer your questions about what these tests are, the information they provide, and how it is used.

What is a standardized achievement test? What tests is your child required to take?

A standardized achievement test is simply a test that is developed using standard procedures and administered and scored in a consistent manner for all test takers. Students respond to identical or very similar questions under the same conditions and test directions. The standardization of test questions, directions, conditions of testing, and scoring is needed to make test scores comparable and to assure, as much as possible, that test takers have equal, unbiased opportunities to demonstrate what they know and what they can do. In contrast, classroom and teacher-developed tests are not considered to be standardized because they vary in content, are not given under identical conditions, and are scored using variable rules.

What do standardized tests look like? The most common tests include one or both of these formats:

- **Multiple-choice questions.** Many standardized tests require students to select a single correct response to each test question from a small number of options and to mark their choice on an answer sheet.

- **Performance assessment questions.** These require students to give the answer to a question without choosing from a set of provided responses. With written-response questions, the most commonly used performance assessments, students fill in a blank or provide a brief written response to a question. Other examples of performance assessments include demonstrations, exhibitions, journals, and portfolios. (These are also known as *authentic assessments*. See pages 148–149.) Performance assessments can be given and scored according to standard procedures and rules so that a test containing performance assessment questions is a standardized test. These more elaborate assessments are far less widely used than the multiple-choice or written-response variety, owing to time and money constraints.

Your child must take annual standardized tests in reading/language arts and mathematics in each of grades 3–8 and at least once in grades 10–12. Beginning in the 2007–08 school year, your child is also required to take a standardized science assessment at least once in each of three grade spans: 3–5, 6–9, and 10–12. These tests, which are required under the No Child Left Behind Act (NCLB), are developed and administered at the state level. Some states also administer more extensive assessments. They may begin standardized testing earlier than third grade, administer testing in every grade level, or include social studies testing in their assessments. The pattern varies across the country.

Your child may also be involved in the National Assessment of Educational Progress (NAEP), called "The Nation's Report Card." This is the only national-level assessment of what students in the United States know and can do in various academic subjects. NAEP administers reading and mathematics tests every two years, and it tests other subjects in alternate years. NAEP does not report scores for individual students or schools; instead, it provides data regarding subject matter achievement, instructional experiences, and overall school environment for populations of students (for example, fourth graders) and groups within those populations (for example, Hispanic students). Although states are not required to take part in NAEP, around forty generally do so per year. In a typical state, 100 schools are selected in each of grades four, eight, and twelve to represent the state's demographic and geographic composition.

Within a selected school and grade, twenty-five to thirty students are chosen for each subject tested. All of the data collected from selected students in all the schools are then combined to represent all students in the state. So if your child is selected to take this test, understand that he was randomly selected to participate. You will not get to see his test results, since they are not reported individually. Unlike the state-required standardized tests that your child takes, which can be quite lengthy, NAEP assessments normally take less than ninety minutes.

What is the difference between a criterion-referenced test and a norm-referenced test?

A criterion-referenced test (CRT) measures your child's performance against a set body of content. State tests that match state standards (also known as standards-based tests) are criterion-referenced tests: they are designed to measure how well your child has learned a specific body of knowledge and skills. Think of the multiple-choice test that you take to get a driver's license and the on-the-road driving test that follows. Both are examples of criterion-referenced tests. Just as it is possible for all examinees to pass driving tests—if they know about driving rules and drive reasonably well—so, too, is it possible for all students taking a CRT to earn a passing grade.

Normally, CRTs are created to determine whether your child has learned the material taught in a specific grade or course. For example, "The student has demonstrated mastery of reading at the third-grade level" is a determination made by a criterion-referenced test. On a standardized CRT, a committee of experts sets the passing score. NCLB requires each state to establish its own unique set of standards for reading, math, and science along with performance standards that define how much of the content standards students should know to reach the basic, proficient, or advanced level in the subject area. In order to measure student mastery of these standards, each state must also design its own assessments according to quality guidelines set out by the United States Department of Education. These assessments must be aligned with the state's academic standards of learning and must provide accurate and consistent information about the student's attainment of the standards, using the performance standards it has defined.

A norm-referenced test (NRT), by contrast, is designed to compare test takers to one another. On an NRT driving test, you would be compared with other test takers as to who knew most or least about driving rules or who drove better or worse. Scores would be reported as a percentage rank, with half of the test takers scoring above a midpoint and half below it. In a similar manner, NRTs compare your child's score against the scores of a group of students, called the *norming group,* who have already taken the same exam.

How does this work? If your child is in sixth grade, test makers select a sample from sixth graders and the test is *normed* on this sample. This is supposed to represent fairly the entire target population—all sixth graders in the nation. Your child's score is then reported in relation to the scores of this norming group.

When you see scores in the paper that report a school's score as a percentile ("the Walter Johnson School ranked at the 45th percentile") or when you see your child's score reported that way ("Maria scored at the 82nd percentile"), the test is probably an NRT. The scores range from 1st percentile to 99th percentile, with the average student score set at the 50th percentile. This means that if Maria scored at the 82nd percentile on the sixth-grade reading test, she scored higher than 82 percent of the test takers in the norming group. The test shows that she reads better than 82 percent of sixth-grade students nationally.

Your child's score on a criterion-referenced test using local academic standards is intended to be compared only with the criteria and your child's own previous scores. By contrast, your child's scores on a norm-referenced test can enable comparisons with other students locally or nationally who have taken the same test.

? What is a high-stakes test?

Some of the tests your child takes in school will be high-stakes tests. These are tests that districts and schools use to make important decisions that affect your child's future, such as her promotion to the next grade level or graduation from high school. High school graduation exams are in place in nearly half the states, and more than half the nation's high school students are required to pass them in order to earn a diploma. School districts and schools also use high-stakes test results to identify children who will receive specialized services such as special education or gifted and talented programming.

It's reasonable for test results to be used as one factor in making high-stakes decisions, but you should be concerned if they are the *only* factor being considered. Tests are a necessary means, but not the exclusive means, to evaluate your child's achievement and growth in skills. Tests are best employed in conjunction with other important types of information, including teacher evaluations of your child's work and classroom performance and other individual and group assessments to measure achievement and growth. These might include, for example:

- a portfolio of written work for English
- paintings or ceramics created in art class
- the memorization and performance of a speech or poem in Italian for foreign language class
- other classroom assessments such as tests and quizzes created by the teacher

High-stakes testing not only affects your child individually, but also can have an impact on your child's school as a whole. That's because, under NCLB, schools have to make adequate yearly progress (AYP) as defined by the state. If a school's actual achievement is at or above the state goal in a given year, the school is designated as making AYP. If achievement is below the goal for two consecutive years, the school is designated as needing improvement. The only assessments used to determine AYP are the state standardized tests, making them very high-stakes indeed!

What types of information can standardized test scores provide? How are the scores used?

Standardized test scores provide information on individual student or group performance that can be interpreted and used in many different ways. Scores are issued on a statewide, districtwide, schoolwide, and individual basis. All scores are made available to the public except those of an individual student or class.

The uses of standardized test scores may include:

- **Identifying the instructional needs of individual students.** A test may be used to diagnose a student's strengths and weaknesses, allowing the teacher at the school to choose effective instructional programs for that student.

- **Giving principals and teachers feedback** to help them target areas where they may need to implement professional development.

- **Demonstrating students' proficiency** in basic skills and their ability to meet academic standards. Test results are used to demonstrate individual student mastery of specific levels of achievement. These determinations can help you see exactly where your child stands in relation to the standards for his grade.

- **Determining student placement.** A student's test scores may be used to determine whether he is required to repeat a grade, or be placed in a specific program or class, or be permitted to graduate from high school.

- **Informing the public about school and student performance.** States administer standardized assessments and report the results, in part, to inform the public about how well the schools are progressing over time and how they compare to other localities and schools. The reports can be used to motivate education reform by influencing parents to take action to improve the quality of their schools.

■ **Holding schools accountable for student performance**
on tests aligned to standards. Under NCLB, consequences
are often attached to test results; these may include school
improvement plans, technical assistance, increased or
decreased funding for schools, and loss of accreditation.

When you look at your child's individual score, you want to
know what it means. Obviously an *advanced* score means that
your child knows the basic subject matter and possesses sound
test-taking skills. Whether it means much more beyond this
depends on the overall integrity of the test. By the same token, a
below basic score probably means that your child does not have
a good grasp of the basic subject matter and may not possess
good test-taking skills.

School districts generally make every effort to help you interpret your child's test scores. They strive to define terms like *basic*
and *proficient* and relate them to specific standards. If you are not
sure what a test score means, do not hesitate to ask the district for
more help.

What can standardized tests *not* do?

Standardized tests don't necessarily provide teachers with information about students that they do not already possess. With few
exceptions, the children who score well are already known by their
teachers to have those capabilities, and those who perform poorly
have generally already been identified as having some academic
difficulties.

The tests themselves have limitations. First of all, tests aren't
precision instruments. Every large-scale test has a "standard error
of measurement" similar to the margin of error in an opinion poll.
Second, a test is but a sampling of all possible questions that could
be asked about a subject. No matter how well designed, a test that
lasts a few hours can't possibly address all the important topics,
concepts, or skills in a broad subject like math. Another issue is
that yearly changes in student population can cause fluctuations
in the average test scores of a class or school. As teachers know
well, each year's class contains a unique mix of students; characteristics such as personality, behavior, socioeconomic background,

language acquisition, and achievement level can all make a huge difference.

Interestingly, there is virtually no use of computer-scored standardized tests throughout Europe. Instead, European countries employ essay-based examinations and oral tests. Denmark, academically one of the highest-scoring countries in the world on international comparisons, has no standardized testing program as it is understood in the United States. While the European approach seems unlikely to materialize in the U.S., it serves as a reminder to keep the testing process in perspective and to balance it with all the other aspects of what your child's school is about. Check for yourself what your child knows and can do. Talking to teachers and looking at actual work samples over time will give you a far better sense of how your child is progressing than will a single test score. Most important, your *child* needs to know how she is doing based on her overall performance at school, not solely on a standardized test score.

The Testing Controversy

It is impossible to discuss the use of standardized tests without mentioning some of the controversy surrounding them. Many critics argue that the emphasis on testing brought about by NCLB reduces teachers to little more than drill sergeants and eliminates from the curriculum anything not likely to appear on a standardized test. Other critics worry that standardized tests may be used as the only criteria to measure a student's competence. They point out that, just as any artist can put on a sub-par performance or any sports team can have an off game, so can any student have a bad test day.

Driven by such concerns, one parent activist group, the Coalition for Authentic Reform in Education (CARE), collected about 15,000 signatures for a petition aimed against the Massachusetts Comprehensive Assessment System (MCAS), which tests children from third grade through high school graduation. A group of teachers in Florida actually tore up bonus checks they received for increasing student scores on the Florida Comprehensive Assessment Test, which awards schools letter grades and cash bonuses for student performance.

Teachers, administrators, and other education experts weigh in on all sides of the testing question. "Assessment is critical," states the principal of an elementary school in Santa Ana, California. "We need assessments to determine if our students have been learning successfully and whether they are ready to go on to the next grade." "It's true that academics are important," says a first-grade teacher from Fort Worth, Texas, "but there's also the feeling that there's more breadth than depth in teaching now." Michele Forman, the 2001 Teacher of the Year, has publicly expressed her concerns about testing, stating, "If anything concerns me, it's the oversimplification of something as complex as assessment. My fear is that learning is becoming standardized. Learning is idiosyncratic. Learning and teaching is messy stuff. It doesn't fit into bubbles."[1] "Tests measure achievement, but they do not give schools a roadmap to improvement," notes a former California school superintendent. "I can get on the scale and it'll tell me how much I weigh; that part's easy. But if I don't analyze how I got to that weight, I don't think it helps me change my behavior."

In an emphatic stand against the misuse of testing, W. James Popham, Professor of Education at the University of California at Los Angeles, states, "When parents try to judge a school's educational quality by using standardized achievement tests, they really are trying to measure temperature with a tablespoon. It's the right job, but the wrong assessment tool."[2] But in a report for the Center on Education Policy, researcher Nancy Kober concludes: "Tests are an indispensable tool in the measurement toolbox. Good tests can provide consistent, comparable, and useful information about student achievement not easily obtained through other means. But tests aren't perfect. Several factors unrelated to learning can cause test scores to fluctuate at the individual or aggregate levels. Consequently, test scores don't always mean what many people think they mean."[3]

In short, while most parents and educators agree that leaving no child behind is a laudable goal and that tests have a role to play in this effort, how this goal is being attained continues to be the subject of much research and debate.

What should you ask your child's principal about testing?

Here's a sampling of some questions you may want to ask:

- How much classroom time will be devoted to preparation for standardized tests?

- Have content areas that are not subject to standardized testing been scaled back or eliminated to allow more time for test preparation? If so, which areas?

- How much attention is the school giving to group activities that promote social development, cooperation, and empathy skills?

- How is the material my child learns in class related to what is covered on tests?

- How will the teacher and the school use the results of federally mandated tests?

- What other means of evaluation will my child's teachers use to measure my child's performance?

- Have tests been integrated into school life in a comfortable manner? Is support available for students whose nervousness may affect performance?

- What safeguards are in place to prevent cheating? Are the rules about cheating clear and explicitly communicated to teachers, parents, and students?

How can the teacher help your child do well on standardized tests?

When it comes to standardized tests, being informed and prepared is the best way to go. There's no doubt that if your child knows what to expect on a test, it will help him enormously. In addition to daily instruction in both content and thinking skills, here are things you want your child's teacher to be doing at school:

- giving students practice tests that include time limits and the format of the standardized test

- helping students learn how to budget their time during a test
- instructing students on how to read test passages carefully
- developing strategies for checking test answers
- involving students in discussion of the intent and purpose of the test
- incorporating test-taking skills throughout the school year and employing them in regular instruction

Test taking today has become an art in itself. It's no longer enough to know the material well. Youngsters also need practice in test-taking skills if they are to do well. Thankfully, most teachers recognize this and work to incorporate such practice into their regular classroom routine.

? What can you do to help your child do well on standardized tests?

With all the pressure surrounding tests, it's understandable if both you and your child feel nervous about them. But you can do some things to ease the tension. Here are some great ideas to help your child go into a test feeling prepared and confident:

- Read to your child early and often, and encourage her to read on her own. A good vocabulary is essential for passing most standardized tests.
- Learn everything you can about the test your child will be taking.
- Watch for anxious behaviors, like staying up late to cram or being too worried to eat properly.
- Acknowledge that tests are stressful while emphasizing that, with preparation, your child will be ready for the challenge.
- Make sure your child gets enough sleep the night before the test, and send her off with a good breakfast. Avoid any conflicts on the morning of the test.
- Assure your child that if she does her best, both you and she can be satisfied.

Finally, if you have a child with high test anxiety, consider extra outside help. Some schools and many private tutoring agencies offer test preparation tutoring that can be beneficial for children who need help developing test-taking skills and strategies.

How should you react to your child's test scores?

It's natural for both you and your child to feel anxious about receiving the report of his test scores. And it doesn't help matters that you may have to wait several months for those results, depending on where you live. So, as you open that envelope, keep these things in mind:

- Criterion-referenced tests (CRTs) and norm-referenced tests (NRTs) give you two different types of information about your child.

- How you respond to your child and his test scores can have a significant impact on how he feels about himself. If the scores are lower than you or he expected, try to react in a calm, comforting manner, remembering that one bad test day should not define your child's academic career.

- If you are concerned about your child's scores and feel they do not accurately reflect his abilities, make an appointment with the teacher. The teacher knows how your child has done on homework, projects, quizzes, and tests, and can give you the big picture. As mentioned earlier, standardized test scores generally do not reveal more about your child than the teacher already knows.

- If your child hasn't been doing well in school but brings home high test scores, it may be that he isn't working to the best of his ability in school. At your appointment with the teacher, ask if the standardized test results are consistent with your child's performance in the classroom. If they are not, discuss how you can all work together to change this.

- Overall, avoid putting too much emphasis on standardized tests. A test is only one piece of a puzzle, and there are myriad reasons why your child may not have done well on a particular day. However, if the pattern of low scores continues over a period of time, then it's time to check out what's going on.

What are authentic assessments?

A growing number of states are using alternative assessments, sometimes called authentic assessments or performance assessments. These include essay tests, portfolios, demonstration projects, experiments, service learning, and other work projects that measure a student's ability to do an actual task. In authentic assessments, students use remembered information to produce an original product, participate in a performance, or complete a process. For example, a group of students at a school in North Carolina became involved in the development of an electric-powered vehicle, applying their math, science, and physics learning to the vehicle's design and construction. Playing a piece of music, delivering a dramatic monologue, and conducting a chemistry experiment are other examples. Students are assessed according to specific criteria, or *rubrics*, that are known to them in advance. Rubrics can help students understand the strengths and weaknesses of their work better than they could with a simple letter grade.

Another example of authentic assessment is the portfolio, a systematic collection of a student's work, used as part of a standardized assessment system or by an individual teacher as part of ongoing classroom grading. Artists, photographers, models, and architects have used portfolios for years. An important feature of portfolios is that they can be updated as your child's skills and achievements grow. Portfolio assessment refers to the evaluation of your child's evolving achievements by appraising a collection of her work samples assembled over a period of time. Most educators and parents who advocate portfolio assessment contend that its chief virtues are the promotion of students' self-evaluation capabilities, stimulated by their personal ownership of their portfolios.

Of course, implementing a portfolio assessment program in the classroom represents a significant commitment of teachers' time, and so not all teachers embrace it. As with other aspects of teaching, not all teachers' personalities and instructional styles are well suited to this form of classroom testing. Not all types of classes lend themselves to portfolio assessment, either. But with the right teacher and the right class, it can be of tremendous benefit to your child.

These alternative assessments do not indicate a reduction of academic rigor or standards. You probably remember from your days in the classroom that it can be much more difficult to write a paper, conduct and demonstrate an experiment, or assemble a portfolio of work than to take a test on a single day at school.

Reaction against multiple-choice standardized testing is one reason authentic assessments are gaining momentum in some settings. Teachers, students, and parents know that thoughtfully designed and implemented tests are an integral part of the learning process. They understand that standardized tests can provide valuable information on how well students are achieving and on how to improve student performance. When such tests are in place, the system works well. However, due to the workload involved in producing a number of standardized tests in a short time, budgetary concerns, the presence of high-stakes tests, and pressure from school boards and superintendents, not all state tests are perfectly aligned to their standards. Some states, in fact, simply do not have the funds to cover both the every-year assessment requirements of NCLB and the development of additional, more sophisticated tests.

Many teachers, too, feel pressured to have their students do well on tests, and this has resulted in teachers presenting knowledge solely as a testing goal. Obviously, this is not the intent of the test makers. Nevertheless, in response to this "teaching to the test" phenomenon, educators are advocating the use of authentic performance assessments that promote high levels of achievement and simultaneously keep the process centered on the student and on learning itself.

Returning to the basics about testing: No test should ever be used as the *only* measurement of your child's progress. It can be difficult, too, to remember that many of the things that matter most to you as a parent, to employers, and to community members—good citizenship, how people treat one another, and moral excellence—cannot be well assessed by any of the tools just described. So, perhaps another question to ask of schools is, "What are you doing to promote character, emotional intelligence, and people skills, and how are you assessing the students' progress in these areas?"

What about IQ tests?

IQ stands for *intelligence quotient.* IQ tests measure ability or aptitude rather than achievement; they are designed to assess your child's *capacity* for learning. There are a few reasons you may wish to request an IQ test for your child: On the one hand, if your child is bored and not challenged by his current classroom activities, but his teachers do not recognize his level of achievement, you may need to provide documentation of his potential by means of an IQ test. Likewise, if there are educational opportunities that are available only to students with a demonstrated level of aptitude, such as an advanced math or language arts program, and you want your child to be offered these opportunities, you may wish to request an IQ test. On the other hand, if you are concerned that your child seems to be performing well below his peers academically, an IQ test can determine whether your child's intellectual development is lower than what is normal for children his age or if he really is underachieving. The pattern of strengths and weaknesses reflected in an IQ test may also help to determine if your child has a specific learning disability. A word of caution: an IQ score alone does not determine a student's needs, an appropriate curriculum, or what program a school district may offer to meet those needs.

Your child's IQ is a score on a series of tests that measure cognitive ability (usually verbal and mathematical skills). An IQ score tells you what your child's rank is on a particular intelligence test compared to other test takers in his age group. The developers of IQ tests use mathematical calculations to find the average *(mean)* score. An IQ score from 90 to 110 is generally considered average, corresponding to roughly the middle 50 percent of the population. At the high end, 2 to 3 percent of the population have IQ scores above 130. An IQ score of 145 should occur 0.1 percent of the time, or one time in 1,000. Children with an IQ of 130 or higher are generally designated as gifted in most school districts that identify students of advanced abilities. However, some districts have a higher cutoff for gifted programs, such as an IQ of 140. Generally, if a student has an IQ score below 70, the school or district places the child in a classroom for students with developmental delays.

Although individualized intelligence tests take considerable time to administer and interpret, they provide better information than group intelligence tests, which often underestimate the scores received on individual tests. Thus, if you are considering having your child assessed, request that a school psychologist administer an individualized test. The best and most widely used individual IQ tests for school-age children are the Wechsler Intelligence Scale for Children, Third Edition (WISC-III) and the Stanford Binet Intelligence Test, Fourth Edition (SB-IV).

There are, of course, some cautions about IQ tests. First, IQ scores only give information about one specific facet of intelligence as displayed in children who excel in verbal and logical thinking in the most traditional sense, often called general intellectual ability. Thus, of the forty-nine states that have policies regarding gifted education, every state includes general intelligence ability as *one* type of giftedness to be identified. IQ score alone does not determine a student's academic needs or what programs a school district might offer to meet those needs.

Second—and importantly—while assessments, including IQ tests, should be utilized to obtain important information that can be used for educational planning, they should never be used for labeling, either pejoratively or positively. As a parent, before you request an IQ test, you can make sure that the information gained will be used to set up appropriate educational interventions for your child and not to label him.

Finally, an IQ score reveals a student's innate ability to reason and capacity to learn, but the score is not a crystal ball predicting the future. Academic success involves many other factors besides cognitive intelligence. IQ tests do not measure creativity, leadership, initiative, curiosity, artistic or musical talent, or social and emotional progress.

Where can you find out more?

The National Education Association (page 19) and the U.S. Department of Education (page 135) offer detailed information on standardized testing and NCLB. Here are additional resources to help demystify standardized testing:

National Center for Fair and Open Testing (FairTest)
342 Broadway
Cambridge, MA 02139
617-864-4810
www.fairtest.org
This organization works to end the misuses of standardized testing and to ensure that the evaluation of students, teachers, and schools is fair, open, valid, and educationally beneficial.

Testing! Testing! What Every Parent Should Know About School Tests by W. James Popham (Boston: Allyn & Bacon, 2000) is an invaluable guide to every type of school testing.

Chapter Notes

1. Public statement by Michele Forman, 2001 Teacher of the Year, at a White House ceremony April 23, 2001.

2. Popham, W. James, *Testing! Testing! What Every Parent Should Know About School Tests* (Allyn & Bacon, 2000), p. 66.

3. Center on Education Policy, "What Tests Can and Cannot Tell Us" by Nancy Kober, with Naomi Chudowsky and Diane Stark Rentner, in *TestTalk for Leaders*, issue 2, October 2002.

YOUR RIGHTS AS A PARENT

The majority of public schools in the United States welcome parental input. They recognize that educating children is a three-way affair, centered on the pivotal triangle of the children, their parents, and the school. As a parent, it's important for you to understand what your rights are with respect to your child's education so that you can effectively play your part. While you may never have to exercise all these rights, knowing that you have them is another reminder of the importance of your role as a parent. Knowledge is power!

? Can you stop by school to observe your child's class?

Visiting your child's classroom when school is in session—not just at parent-teacher conferences—is an excellent way to understand your child's school experience. Parents and guardians of enrolled students have the right to be included in the educational process and to have access to the system on behalf of their children. So, visit! But get prior approval before stopping by. Arrange the date and time in advance with both the school office and the teacher.

When you visit during the regular school day, expect to sign in and maybe even receive a name tag to wear during your visit. Don't be intimidated by office staff who guard their school with vigilance. They are only doing their job to protect students, including your child, from potential harm. A strict "Welcome to Everglade Elementary School—please sign in" is the sort of greeting you actually *want* when you visit your child's school.

Once inside the school, you are under the jurisdiction of the building principal who has the responsibility to develop rules and procedures that maintain a safe and orderly learning environment. Principals can choose to limit the frequency and duration of any visit to avoid distraction to the teacher's schedule and classroom atmosphere.

Ask at your school front office for any further specific regulations. Many schools require that the parent or guardian be the only visitor in the classroom during the observation. If you want to bring somebody else with you, you will probably need to get the principal's consent. She or he may want to accompany you during the observation, and this will make it easier to ask any questions that arise.

One final note: As a guest of the school, you will be expected to respect all aspects of individual student confidentiality— something you would want for your own child. You may, for example, observe the teacher disciplining a student who is causing problems or notice quiz scores of your child's classmates. Keep this kind of knowledge to yourself.

? Who has access to your child's permanent record? What if it contains inaccurate information?

Your child's file is a record of her school history. Teachers, counselors, or district staff review these records before recommending placement and making other decisions concerning your child. The Family Educational Rights and Privacy Act (FERPA), passed in 1974, permits you to read the file that the school maintains on your child. FERPA is a federal law that protects the privacy of student education records and also gives you the right to do the following:

- **Inspect and review your child's education records** maintained by the school. If you are a divorced parent and do not have custody of your child, you still have this same right to inspect her school records. However, schools are not required to provide *copies* of records, unless it is impossible for parents to review the records in person. Note that if this is the case, the school will probably ask you to fill out a request form, and it may charge a fee for copies.

▨ **Request that the school correct records** that you believe to be inaccurate or misleading. If your school decides not to amend the record, you have the right to a formal hearing. After the hearing, if the school still decides not to amend the record, you can place a statement in the record setting forth your view about the contested information.

Schools are required to notify parents annually of their rights under FERPA. Notification might come in a special letter, a PTA bulletin, the student handbook, or the local newspaper.

The information in your child's permanent file is confidential and should be kept under lock and key. Generally, schools must have written permission from a parent in order to release any information from a student's education record. However, FERPA allows schools to disclose those records without consent to the following parties and under the following conditions:

▨ school officials with legitimate educational interest

▨ other schools to which a student is transferring

▨ specified officials for audit or evaluation purposes

▨ appropriate parties in connection with financial aid to a student

▨ organizations conducting certain studies on behalf of the school

▨ accrediting organizations

▨ officers of the court to comply with a judicial order or subpoena

▨ appropriate officials in cases of health and safety emergencies

▨ state and local authorities within a juvenile justice system

What information is in the file?
Why should you review it?

You may be amazed at the amount of information in your child's file: copies of report cards and progress reports; your child's scores on standardized tests and any districtwide tests; test results and evaluations used to determine your child's placement in a program for gifted children, a special education program, or bilingual classes; a record of attendance and medical history; notes from placement hearings and appeals; extracurricular activities and honors; your child's discipline record, if any; and a log of everyone other than teachers or counselors who has requested information and the reasons for so doing. If you have given your consent to allow people other than your child's teachers and counselors to read the file, that information also should be there.

You may also discover nonschool-related information in the file. For example, some schools place court information in a student's file. However, attorneys with the United States Department of Education suggest that if there are court records, they should be maintained in a sealed envelope. A permanent education record should contain only information that could benefit the student's education.

Check out your child's permanent record periodically just to make sure it is in good order. Definitely review the file if your child is graduating, transferring to a new district, being considered for special education or gifted programming, or having any kind of problem at school. After reviewing the file, request that the school remove, or at least correct, any kind of misleading information. And add any material that you feel will help new teachers better appreciate your child: for example, reference to a special award earned outside of school or a recommendation from a former teacher.

Can the school publish your
personal information in a directory?

Under FERPA, schools may release what's known as *directory information* to employers, potential employers, the media, private schools, colleges, and the military unless you protest or your school has passed a policy against releasing information to outsiders. Each school district has the authority to decide what information will be distributed and which groups will receive it. In general, school information includes a student's name, address, telephone number, date and place of birth, honors and awards, and dates of attendance.

Before releasing any directory information, the school must let parents know the type of information to be released and the groups that are eligible to receive it. If you do not want the school to disclose any particular information—or any information at all—about your child, you will need to send a written request to the school.

On the other hand, it may be that you would like access to some of this information yourself. For example, if you or a group of parents are trying to organize some after-school classes at your school, you may want to mail information to parents and follow up with a phone call or email. Federal law does not prevent a school district from releasing directory information as long as parents are notified ahead of time. In practice, most districts leave this for individual schools to decide.

It's possible that your principal will refuse to grant permission to release directory information, claiming that this is a violation of family privacy rights. In such a case, ask the school to include a check-off box on next year's parent contact information form stating that the parent gives permission to the school to release the information to parents and other members of the school community. There are good reasons why a principal may be nervous about releasing such information, so don't be surprised if yours is reluctant to do so. If the principal does agree, he or she is likely to insist that you not use the information for nonschool purposes yourself or share it with a third party, such as a realtor or an insurance agent.

What rights do you have if your child has a learning disability?

Before the Education of All Handicapped Children Act was passed in 1975, followed by the Individuals with Disabilities Education Act (IDEA) in 1991, parents of children with disabilities had no legal rights. Schools could decide whether to place children in special education and how long to keep them there. Not only were parents denied the opportunity to have a say in what happened to their children, schools didn't even have to inform parents when such decisions were made.

This has all changed. Today parents have a wide range of rights. With the passage of IDEA and subsequent amendments came the fundamental provision of the right of parents of children with disabilities to participate in the educational decision-making process. This includes the right to:

- Receive a free appropriate education for your child—an education that meets the unique educational needs of your child at no extra cost to you.

- Have your child educated in the least restrictive environment possible. This means the school should make every effort to develop an educational program that will provide the services and supports your child needs in order to be *mainstreamed*—taught with children who do not have disabilities.

- Request an evaluation if you think your child needs special education or related services.

- Be notified when the school wants to evaluate your child or change his placement.

- Request a reevaluation if you believe your child's placement is no longer appropriate. (The school must reevaluate your child at least every three years, but his educational program must be reviewed at least once during each educational year.)

- Obtain another, independent evaluation if you disagree with the school's evaluation.

- Have your child tested in the language he knows best. (Also, students who are hearing impaired have the right to an interpreter during the testing.)

- Review all of your child's educational records.

- Participate in the development of your child's Individualized Education Program (IEP).

- Be kept informed about your child's progress at least as often as parents of children who do not have disabilities.

- Request a due process hearing to resolve differences with the school.

When you have concerns about your child's rights, address them with his classroom teacher and special education service providers. If these efforts aren't successful, or if you believe that your rights or your child's rights have been violated, bring the matter up as soon as possible with the appropriate school administrator. If you are not satisfied with the administrator's response, contact the special education branch of your state Department of Education. Ask for the name of a special education advocate to help you work with your school. Most states have advocacy agencies that can provide you with the guidance you need to pursue your case at no cost. You also can try finding a suitable advocate by locating a state or regional nonprofit advocacy group working in the area of your child's disability. (See pages 163–164 and 175–177 for advocacy organizations.)

What if the school suggests medication for your child?

The decision to place a child on any kind of prescription medication can only be made by a physician and with parental consent. However, a school can suggest that you seek a medical evaluation for your child. How should you respond if this happens? First of all, listen carefully to what your child's teachers have observed, but recognize that the classic symptoms of a condition like Attention Deficit Hyperactivity Disorder (ADHD), for example, can be due to a variety of other causes. If your school has approached you about a problem with your child, be sure to visit the class and observe her yourself and request that a specialist observe her. Afterward, meet with your child's teachers and counselors to gather and share information. Finally, take your child to a trained and experienced clinician—one who will carefully assess her development, family history, and behavior at school and at home—to make a thorough medical diagnosis. Ask your pediatrician for a referral or, if possible, seek out a fellow parent who has successfully used the services of such a professional.

To be diagnosed with ADHD*, your child should display a significant number of symptoms and behaviors reflecting hyperactivity, impulsivity, and inattention. These symptoms and behaviors

---

*ADHD is mentioned as an example because children diagnosed with ADHD often take medication as part of their treatment.

must be more persistent and severe than those that normally occur in children your child's age. There must also be impaired functioning in school, at home, or in social relationships. After a diagnosis of ADHD, your doctor will be able to discuss a comprehensive program for addressing your child's issues, a program which may include medication and other interventions. Even if medications are prescribed, they should rarely, if ever, be the only treatment your child receives. And, most importantly, whatever the diagnosis, only *you* have the legal right to make the decision as to the best course of action for your child. The school cannot require that your child take any kind of medication as a condition of enrollment.

What are your rights if your child gets into trouble at school?

All parents hope they never have to become too personally familiar with their school's discipline policy. But children do misbehave sometimes. If this happens, you will want to be sure that your child is being treated fairly. Most school discipline issues are handled within school, often with a phone call home so that parents know what is going on. Older forms of school discipline often involved the birch or the cane, but a growing opposition to corporal punishment has mostly forced out such treatment. (Not completely, though. See pages 161–163 for more information on corporal punishment.) Today educators generally advocate a disciplinary policy focused on giving positive reinforcement and rewarding good behavior. When this does not work, most schools have in place disciplinary policies that include in-school detentions, peer counseling, and conflict mediation. Whatever the method, the goal is to teach self-discipline rather than rely on outside controls. At the same time, out-of-school suspensions or expulsions have become much more common as zero tolerance policies have been implemented over concerns for children's safety.

Each state, and sometimes even each school district, has specific guidelines for how a school disciplinary process must be conducted. There are, however, some general principles of federal law that apply to all schools. Students typically can be suspended or expelled for:

- possession of alcohol, other drugs, or weapons

- assaulting other students

- repeated disruptive behavior

Since education at a public elementary, middle, and high school is a constitutionally protected right, your child must be allowed *due process* before he can be suspended or expelled. What does this mean?

- You and your child have the right to know the school's rules ahead of time. Most schools publish behavior rules in student handbooks and distribute them to students at the beginning of each year. They also may be posted at the school. If your child's school has not made the rules available to you or him, you may be able to argue that he didn't know about the rule he was violating.

- You must receive adequate notice of the charges against your child, either verbally or in writing. The information should include the specific act involved, a description of the evidence the school is relying on, and the exact number of days of suspension and the dates it will be imposed.

- In addition, you have the right to appear and challenge the suspension or expulsion. You should be given a specific date, time, and location for such a hearing. At the appeals hearing, school representatives will present the evidence against your child, and you will be able to speak in your child's defense.

- In some states, you will also receive information about programs that might help improve your child's behavior.

Services for a student who has a diagnosed emotional or behavioral disorder are included under IDEA. See Chapter 11 to learn more.

What can you do if a school official paddles your child? Isn't that against the law?

Since the 1970s, the use of corporal punishment in the U.S. has declined. More than half the states have banned it. In parts of the country, however, paddling is legal in public schools.

If you live in a state that permits paddling and your school practices it, understand that both state laws and local policies determine how it can be applied. If you object to the practice of paddling and your child has been spanked at school, ask for a copy of the paddling policy from your school board to see if the school official involved followed the required procedures. If you find that the official did not act legally and in accordance with school policies, make an appointment with the district superintendent and ask that the official be reprimanded or dismissed. Even if correct procedures were followed but you remain concerned over the policy, seek a waiver for your child by writing a letter asking that your child *not* be physically punished, and ask your family healthcare provider to cosign it. At the same time, comfort your child. Explain that you believe no one has a right to hit another person and that she should not have been hit. Your child may be reluctant to speak about the incident, perhaps out of fear that you will blame her, so let her know that you want to be told whenever this occurs.

What if a teacher forcibly pulls a child by the arm? Is this corporal punishment? Regardless of whether you live in a state that allows corporal punishment, if you see the teacher grab your child by the arm in an aggressive manner, you should inform the school principal. Ask what the principal will do about it and request that he or she follow up on your concerns. It is important to determine whether this was a one-time event or a regular part of the teacher's classroom management approach. Even if you do not witness the pulling, but your child reports it, you should still make an appointment with the principal. While your child might not have understood exactly what was happening or the teacher's motive, you can still ask the principal to observe the teacher and get back to you.

In the worst-case scenario, if your child suffers an injury from being spanked, take her to an emergency room or a pediatrician. Have colored pictures taken of the injury. If you take the pictures yourself, be sure to have a witness. Ask your physician to report the injury to your local county's Child Protection Services (CPS). Follow up to make sure the physician does so, or do it yourself if necessary. Be sure to keep a written record of everyone you talk to concerning the incident, along with the outcome and the dates of your communications with authorities in case you have to consult a lawyer.

Putting an End to Corporal Punishment in Schools

If you are someone who opposes corporal punishment in schools, you will find plenty of supporters in your camp. Most child-advocacy groups have a position similar to that of the National Association of School Psychologists (NASP), which states, "Corporal punishment negatively affects the social, psychological, and educational development of students and contributes to the cycle of child abuse and pro-violence attitudes of youth."[1] If you feel passionate about this issue, consider organizing support for a ban on corporal punishment in your school district. Chapters 1 and 5 offer ideas on how to work with other parents to influence your school board and state legislature.

Where can you find out more?

The U.S. Department of Education (page 135) has a detailed guide to FERPA that you can order or download. Here are additional resources to help you know and exercise your rights when it comes to your child's education. You'll also want to review the resources regarding special education and learning disabilities on pages 175–177.

American Academy of Pediatrics
141 Northwest Point Boulevard
Elk Grove Village, IL 60007
847-434-4000
www.aap.org
Visit the parent section of the Web site to find links for locating a pediatrician.

Center for Effective Discipline
155 W. Main Street, Suite 1603
Columbus, OH 43215
614-221-8829
www.stophitting.com

This organization is the headquarters for the National Coalition to Abolish Corporal Punishment in Schools and EPOCH-USA (End Physical Punishment of Children).

KidsHealth
www.kidshealth.org
Another source of information on finding a doctor, the parent section of this comprehensive health Web site also offers details on a range of disabilities and medical conditions and on medications and alternative approaches.

National Dissemination Center for Children with Disabilities (NICHCY)
P.O. Box 1492
Washington, DC 20013
800-695-0285
www.nichcy.org
NICHCY provides a wealth of information about learning disabilities, including details about the legal rights of children with learning disabilities and their parents.

The Survival Guide for Kids with ADD or ADHD by John F. Taylor (Minneapolis: Free Spirit Publishing, 2006). Written for kids but full of helpful information for parents, this book addresses medication, diet, behavior, school, and more.

Chapter Notes

1. National Association of School Psychologists, "Position Paper on Corporal Punishment in Schools," July 2006.

SPECIAL EDUCATION CONCERNS

One of the most difficult experiences for parents is to see that their child is different, unlike the other kids. Not fitting in may be painful for your child, and watching it is probably painful for you. The good news is that you and your child are not alone. Plenty of young people, for lots of different reasons, don't match the "regular kid" mold. Many, too, have the benefit of learning early in life the rewards that go with embracing their individuality and facing their unique learning challenges. At school, some students may struggle to read or interact in the classroom because of a learning disability. Others may be so bright that their grasp and breadth of learning is beyond that of other students, or so creative that their whole approach to learning is unique. Behavior issues sometimes relate to these or other conditions and can result in emotional difficulties or problems with social skills.

Many children who face challenges like these receive special education services at school. Students with disabilities receive these services under one of two laws: the Individuals with Disabilities Education Act (IDEA) or Section 504 of the Rehabilitation Act of 1973. Services for gifted students fall under federal, state, and local regulations. This chapter will discuss some of the more common special education situations and give you tools to help your child succeed.

? What if your child has a learning disability or disorder?

Around 14 percent of public schoolchildren in the United States receive special education services.[1] Although this number includes children with speech or language impairments, various health conditions, autism, and severe mental and physical disabilities, many of these youngsters were diagnosed with specific learning disabilities or disorders. Learning disabilities are neurological conditions that interfere with a person's ability to store, process, or produce information. Simply put, if your child has a learning disability, it means that he learns differently and needs to receive different instruction to match the way his brain works. As an example, a child who has difficulty with auditory processing may learn better by using visual aids and hands-on activities. Learning disabilities should not be confused with disabilities that are primarily the result of visual, hearing, or motor handicaps; of mental retardation; of emotional disturbance; or of environmental, cultural or economic disadvantages. Children with learning disabilities generally possess average or above-average intelligence, but there is often a gap between potential and actual achievement. These are "invisible" disabilities, since the child seems perfectly normal yet is unable to perform at the same level as his peers.

Some common learning disabilities and disorders include:

- attention deficit disorder/attention deficit hyperactivity disorder (ADD/ADHD)—problems with impulsivity, inattention, and/or hyperactivity
- auditory processing disorder—difficulty perceiving the differences between speech sounds
- dyslexia—difficulty processing one or more areas of language and reading
- dyscalculia—difficulty comprehending arithmetic and math concepts
- dysgraphia—severe trouble writing legibly and with appropriate speed
- dyspraxia—problems with motor coordination

- language learning disorders—trouble understanding spoken language; poor reading comprehension

- nonverbal learning disorders—trouble with nonverbal cues, such as body language; poor coordination, clumsiness

- visual perception disorders—difficulty noticing and interpreting visual information

Chapter 7 discusses what to do if you see that your child is struggling. If you already have done all that you can in terms of working with the classroom teacher, and you still feel—or the school determines—that your child's situation requires more serious attention, it's time to take the next step in getting to the root of his problem and obtaining the support he needs.

Start by making an appointment with a healthcare professional to rule out vision and auditory problems. If you get the all clear from the specialist, you'll want to go back to your school and request that your child be assessed for learning disabilities. As a parent, you have the right to request this evaluation. Typically, however, the classroom teacher is the person responsible for referring a child for a special education evaluation. This makes sense, because most teachers can tell if a student is floundering in ways unrelated to ability or effort.

Once the referral for your child is in place, a special team is set up to decide if he is eligible for special education services. This team generally consists of your child's teachers, the school counselor and/or psychologist, the school nurse, and perhaps the principal and other specialists. If the team determines that previous accommodations have not worked and a more serious problem remains, the team will follow through and refer your child for a special education assessment.

You must be notified in writing that your child has been referred for this testing, and you must give your written consent for the evaluation to proceed. In most states there is a prescribed time for completing the evaluation after the initial referral has been made, usually within thirty or sixty days.

An assessment specialist such as a school psychologist will administer the tests, which may take several days depending on how many tests your child must take and the amount of time allotted for each testing session. The school should inform you about all aspects of this testing, including what tests will be given, what the school hopes to learn from the tests, how much time each test will take, when the results will be known, and how to interpret the results.

What Goes into Assessment?

Assessment for special education should be as nondiscriminatory as possible. What does this mean? You can expect assessment standards and procedures that:[2]

- use a variety of strategies, tools, and tests to gain information about the student's needs and abilities

- are administered by trained staff in the student's native language or communication mode (such as sign language)

- assess all areas that relate to the suspected disability (such as health, general intelligence, motor skills, school performance, sight and hearing, social skills, and emotional status)

- evaluate cognitive, behavioral, physical, and developmental factors

- are not racially or culturally biased

- are designed and selected to ensure accurate results

- are weighed next to existing information such as parent input, classroom tests, and teacher observations

---

This can be a difficult and stressful time for you, your child, and the rest of your family. You hope nothing serious comes to light, but most of all you just want to know. Meanwhile, your child has to sit through lengthy tests, which may seem to exacerbate learning difficulties. For this reason, it's crucial that you explain to your child that the testing is designed to help him. It will determine how he learns best. The school will then be able to teach him more effectively. As a result, things can change for the better.

Based on the results of the tests administered to your child, plus other informal assessment measures such as family history and teacher observation, a team of experts, probably including the school psychologist, a special education teacher, and the school counselor, decides whether your child is eligible for special education services.

Turning on a Light

In the case of my own child (and indeed numerous other children), the testing was a blessing. Before the tests, Billy knew he couldn't read like the other kids but didn't understand why and couldn't talk about it. Ashamed, he hid in a corner of his classroom, hoping to escape attention. When the psychologist explained that he had dyslexia, a light went on in Billy's head. He was utterly relieved to learn that his inability to read wasn't his fault. Then, for the first time, he began telling me how hard it had been for him to watch other kids reading when he couldn't make the letters stay still on the page. Testing can be an eye-opener for everyone.

If it is determined that your child is eligible for special education services under IDEA, you will be notified in writing and asked to attend a meeting with school personnel to design an educational program for your child. This program is known as the Individualized Education Program or IEP.* Your child's public school is obliged by law to provide all the tools and supplements deemed necessary to keep him learning and to do so, to the maximum extent possible, in the context of the general classroom. The IEP is the plan to make this happen. It is a legal contract between the school and your child stipulating services to be provided, and it must be adhered to.

The shape and direction of the IEP are collaboratively developed in a conference attended by your child's classroom teacher, the school counselor, the resource specialist, possibly the principal or school psychologist, and you, the parent. Parents are partners in this process and are required to sign off on the plan, indicating their approval. Some parents feel intimidated when meeting with so many professionals and hearing lots of technical jargon. Your participation in the IEP process, however, is vital. Together, you and the educators at school are working as a team to give your

---

*An IEP is different from a Section 504 plan as described in Chapter 2. A 504 plan is a legal document falling under the provisions of Section 504 of the Rehabilitation Act of 1973; it does not require that a child be identified as needing special education under IDEA to qualify, and it is generally less sweeping than an IEP. Most, but not all, learning disabilities fall under IDEA.

child the best opportunities to succeed. Keep in mind that you are the expert on your child: you know him better than anyone else and probably have ideas about modifications that will serve him best. If for any reason you feel the need for support as you work with this team, take an outside advocate with you to the IEP meeting. Schools are familiar with this procedure. You simply need to let the school know ahead of time that an advocate will be attending with you. (See pages 175–177 for a list of organizations that can help you find an advocate.)

Once your child is cleared to receive special education services, his progress is evaluated over the course of the school year and reported to you at specific times, typically quarterly. The IEP is an annual document. As such, your child will have an annual meeting to review his progress and to develop a new IEP for the upcoming year. Every three years he will undergo a full reassessment to determine whether he is still eligible for special education. This reevaluation should include any further test results to demonstrate your child's progress over the years. You also can ask for a reevaluation at any time, although an assessment cannot be conducted more frequently than once a year unless both you and the district agree that one is necessary. The reevaluation must be completed, and the report given to you, within sixty school days of the district's receipt of your written request.

Parenting children with learning disabilities presents special challenges and can be emotionally exhausting and stressful for parents. Learning coping strategies is really important for you. It will undoubtedly be helpful to learn what has worked for children with needs similar to your child's. Contacting other parents and advocacy groups is a good way to do this. In the long run, such groups provide an invaluable support system, providing both the skill training and emotional support you need. Besides sharing knowledge and experience, a parent group often can be an effective force on behalf of your child. And you may well find that parents who have been through situations similar to yours become some of your closest friends. (See pages 175–177 for information on finding a parent support group.)

A Word About Preschool and Kindergarten-Age Children

Under IDEA, special education services, including testing, are available at no cost for students from ages 3 to 22 who are educated in public schools. However, formal identification of a child's learning disability generally does not occur until there is a measurable discrepancy between the child's aptitude and academic achievement, often not until the second or third grade.

What if you suspect your 3-, 4-, or 5-year-old has difficulty learning?

- Meet with a pediatrician to express your concerns; ask if developmental screenings are available or if another medical professional (such as a neurologist or speech/language pathologist) should evaluate your child.

- Ask for a referral to the agency you should contact to arrange an evaluation for your child.

Keep in mind that, depending on where you live, preschool services may be available for eligible children with disabilities beginning at age 3. Until age 5, these services are voluntary, meaning that you can decide whether you want to enroll your child in a program that provides special help.

How can you tell if your child is gifted? What services will the school provide?

It used to be the case that being gifted meant that a child tested in the top 5 percent of the population on IQ tests, but educators today understand that giftedness is a lot more than an IQ score. The federal government defines giftedness this way: "Students, children, or youth who give evidence of high achievement capability in areas such as intellectual, creative, artistic, or leadership capacity, or in specific academic fields, and who need services and activities not ordinarily provided by the school in order to fully develop those capabilities."[3] Although states and school districts are not required to use this definition, they generally do so as a basis.

Here are ten generally accepted signs that your child might be gifted:

- advanced intellectual ability
- extensive vocabulary
- intense curiosity
- unusually good memory
- creativity
- high energy
- focus, passion, intensity
- logical and abstract thinking
- heightened sensitivity to the world around her
- remarkable sense of humor

If you believe that your child is gifted, you should bring this to the attention of her teacher. Schools employ different standards of determining giftedness, but identification will most likely be based on one or more of the following:

- group or individualized IQ tests
- standardized achievement tests
- creativity tests
- grades
- teacher observations
- parent recommendation

In making selections for gifted programs, teachers also are urged to look for motivational characteristics, such as whether your child is eager to do extra work and capable of working independently; for creativity, meaning that your child is a strong problem solver and that her work shows originality; and for learning characteristics including advanced vocabulary, consistently high academic performance, and an ability to grasp new concepts quickly.

Sometimes a disability—physical, emotional, or learning-related—can overshadow a gifted child's abilities and talents. In the case of a *twice-exceptional* child, schools may tend to focus on the disability rather than the needs of the whole child. This is another situation where your own personal knowledge of your child is critical. It's important that you advocate for having *all* her special education needs met. A father of a third grader in Clifton, New Jersey, sums it up this way: "Unless you advocate for your child—whether gifted, neurologically typical, or learning disabled in any way—your child will be left behind."

If your school identifies your child as gifted, it will probably place her in a program known as GATE (gifted and talented education) or TAG (talented and gifted), two of the popular acronyms for gifted education. Be aware that school systems often face difficult decisions when seeking to identify gifted children. The amount of money allotted to gifted education must include both identification and programming while providing a balance between the two. With limited funding, some schools make trade-offs between using individual assessments and group measures for gifted identification.

Ideally, information gained during identification will be used to guide curriculum and instruction for your child. You will find that special education for gifted learners can take several forms, depending on your school's budget. Gifted resource or pull-out programs, cluster class grouping, acceleration to the next grade, and single-subject acceleration are most common. It also may simply be up to your child's teacher to make the regular classroom more challenging.

It's important for parents of gifted children to identify their giftedness early on. Experts agree that children's attitudes toward learning are set before age 10. And it can happen that preschool and the early grades turn off gifted kids, who are sometimes told to stop asking so many questions and wait their turn. Gifted kids need an appropriate environment. Without it, seeds for under-achievement may be sown.

Forty-nine states have policies regarding gifted education, but state laws and available funding vary widely, so there is disparity in the services available for gifted and talented students around the country. The fact is that some states spend no money at all on gifted education, and even those that do dispense funds use a range of funding formulas that do not always result in equitable distribution of money. For many states and districts, tough choices have had to be made in terms of helping all students improve under the No Child Left Behind legislation and supporting the needs of exceptionally able or high-achieving students. (This is another call to advocacy for parents of gifted kids!) Check with your state department of education to find out more about gifted and talented education in your state.

? How should you respond if your child is having behavior problems?

Teachers witness a wide range of behavior problems in school, from disruptive talking in the classroom to fighting and name-calling on the playground. In following up these situations, the reasons for problem behavior almost always turn out to be fairly simple: the child is acting out because she has strong feelings about something and doesn't know how to deal with them, or something in school is really not working for her. If your child's teacher calls you about a behavior problem, it may be that the teacher has already tried to intervene with your child, but has not been successful and so needs your help.

When that phone call comes, first ask your child to explain why she is engaging in whatever the specific misbehavior issue is. Try to discover your child's feelings. Really listen to what she says, and don't be quick with a pep talk or a pat on the back. Having some-one to listen, without judging, can help defuse some of your child's frustrations. If she tells you that she is bored, she may be coping with a learning difficulty or perhaps be under-challenged.

Also explore your child's relationship with her teacher. A child who feels the teacher doesn't like her won't be able to learn or behave appropriately. If this is the issue, it may be enough to bring it to the teacher's attention. A foreign language teacher from Kens-ington, Maryland, was astounded when her eighth-grade student broke down in tears over a grade, sobbing, "I know you don't like me, I know you think I'm a bad student." It turned out that due to an incident the previous year, which the student never brought up with anybody, the girl had been sitting in class all year believing that her teacher saw her as "bad." Like most teachers, this teacher was receptive to the child and relieved to understand and be able to work with the student to rectify the misunderstanding. If you believe the teacher actually doesn't like your child and isn't able to work effectively with him, you will want to look into moving your child to a different classroom.

But what if none of these avenues leads to an understanding of what underlies the behavior concerns? Try spending time in your child's classroom to see what's going on. Volunteer as an aide for a day or two. This has the side benefit of allowing you and the teacher to get to know one another, which is always helpful when you need to work together to help your child. While in the classroom, check out your child's learning style and the teacher's teaching style. See if there is a possible communication issue or an expectation that might cause your child to feel misunderstood and act out. On the playground, watch for signs that your child is being teased or frightened and is acting out in an attempt to draw attention to herself.

It may be that your child has a hard time with sitting still and being quiet. In such a case, find out if the teacher is open to letting your child move quietly around the room. Perhaps the teacher will allow him to doodle or draw, as long as he doesn't distract the other children. With older students, I have often been successful by giving them a special task to use up their extra energy. I recall a sixth grader who seemed unable to sit still and never wanted to do any work. Once I made him my assistant, with special responsibilities for taking papers to the principal's office, he changed his attitude.

Finally, it's not unusual for behavior problems to accompany learning problems. Because of this, there are cases where children are identified as having behavioral or emotional disorders and are also eligible to receive some special education services under IDEA or Section 504. This will allow you to work with the school and your child to develop an IEP, a 504 plan, or another program to help your child learn skills and strategies to improve behavior. With the right program and supports in place for your child, behavioral issues should improve.

? Where can you find out more?

The Behavior Survival Guide for Kids by Thomas McIntyre (Minneapolis: Free Spirit Publishing, 2003), is a great resource for children ages 9–14 and parents alike, with information, strategies, and advice geared to students with both diagnosed and general behavior problems.

Families and Advocates Partnership for Education (FAPE)
PACER Center
8161 Normandale Boulevard
Minneapolis, MN 55437
952-838-9000
www.fape.org
FAPE helps parents and advocates improve educational results for children with disabilities. It operates as part of the PACER Center, which works to expand opportunities and enhance the quality of life of children with disabilities and their families, based on the concept of parents helping parents. A great resource for advocacy.

Hoagie's Gifted Education Page
www.hoagiesgifted.org
This Web page provides a variety of resources for gifted youth, parents, and educators.

LD Online
2775 S. Quincy Street
Arlington, VA 22206
703-998-2060
www.ldonline.org
LD Online gives useful information and links to a wealth of resources on learning disabilities.

Learning Disabilities Association of America (LDA)
4156 Library Road
Pittsburgh, PA 15234
412-341-1515
www.ldaamerica.org
This association is a leading source of information about individuals with learning disabilities. The Web site can help you learn about disabilities, advocacy, state chapters, legislative action, and more.

National Association for Gifted Children (NAGC)
1707 L Street NW, Suite 550
Washington, DC 20036
202-785-4268
www.nagc.org
NAGC addresses the unique needs of children and youth with demonstrated gifts and talents. The Web site is a rich source of information with resources on advocacy and legislation and links to state organizations.

National Center for Learning Disabilities (NCLD)
381 Park Avenue South, Suite 1401
New York, NY 10016
888-575-7373
www.ncld.org
This organization is dedicated to providing as much information as possible to parents of children with learning disabilities. In addition, if you are concerned about your young child's reading skills, NCLD has developed an excellent screening tool as part of its online "Get Ready to Read!" program (www.getreadytoread.org) and also has launched the "Recognition & Response" program (www.recognitionandresponse.org), a systematic approach to addressing early learning difficulties before kindergarten.

Schwab Learning
1650 S. Amphlett Boulevard, Suite 300
San Mateo, CA 94402
650-655-2410
www.schwablearning.org
Offers numerous excellent resources to guide parents in helping their children with learning difficulties.

The Survival Guide for Kids with LD by Rhoda Cummings and Gary Fisher (Minneapolis: Free Spirit Publishing, 2002), answers many questions children and parents have. Appropriate for most elementary and middle school students, the book is written at a grade 2.7 reading level.

You Know Your Child Is Gifted When . . . A Beginner's Guide to Life on the Bright Side by Judy Galbraith (Minneapolis: Free Spirit Publishing, 2000), is an excellent and humorous look at characteristics of giftedness and what it means to parent a gifted child.

Chapter Notes

1. Statistics reported in 2006 for the 2003–04 school year by the U.S. Department of Education, National Center for Education Statistics, in "How Many Students with Disabilities Receive Services?"

2. Turnbull et al, *Exceptional Lives: Special Education in Today's Schools,* Fourth Edition (Pearson Education, 2004), pp. 23–24.

3. Definition used in the No Child Left Behind Act (2002), title IX, part A, section 9191(22), p. 544.

OTHER SOURCES OF HELP

In addition to teachers and front office administrators, many other professionals are available to support your child's schooling. Among these are the school nurse, school psychologist, school counselor, and resource specialists in areas such as speech and hearing, reading, learning English, and special education; schools also employ numerous other certified and noncertified personnel. This chapter addresses several of the key functions served by various school professionals.

When will your child visit the school nurse?

Many schools have a nurse or other health technician on staff at least part time; some school districts share nurses, in which case this staffer is on-site only certain hours or days. The school nurse is in charge of the various screenings state law requires public schools to administer, such as those for hearing, vision, and respiratory ailments. The school nurse may also act as a resource for classroom health education and serve on your school's crisis management team. She or he provides emergency assistance for illnesses and injuries sustained at school and is responsible for summoning additional or emergency help when needed. The nurse may also be the person who will call you when your child becomes ill at school.

In most schools, the nurse is responsible for distributing to teachers a list of health concerns for their students. These can range from "slight allergy to pollen" to "allergy to peanuts," "deafness in left ear," or "subject to epileptic seizures." If your child has a health condition or chronic illness such as asthma or diabetes, make it a point to meet with the nurse in person to talk through any information the nurse and other school staff should know.

Children often have to take prescribed daily medications while they are in school, and the school nurse will typically be the person to administer the medication. If there is no nurse on-site, the school's administrative assistant may be the person who handles this. You will need to know and follow school guidelines that grant permission for the designated staffer to administer the medication, and you will probably be required to fill out a form delegating that responsibility. If your child will need medication all year, it's a good idea to have the prescription filled and ready to take to school before the first day along with information describing any other pertinent information: dosage, time to deliver the medicine, possible side effects, and directions on storing the medication properly.

What is the role of the school psychologist?

Perhaps you wonder why you have never met a staff psychologist at your child's school. This may be because, as with a school nurse, your school shares a psychologist with one or more schools in the district. The school psychologist's most important job is to identify and assess any school-related problems a child may be having. You will receive notification if your child is referred to the school psychologist by a teacher or other staff member, and you must give your consent in writing before the psychologist can work with your child.

School psychologists help children and youth succeed academically, socially, and emotionally. They collaborate with educators, parents, and other professionals to create safe, healthy, and supportive learning environments for all students that strengthen connections between home and school. Here are some situations where your child might encounter the school psychologist:

- **Assessment.** When you or your child's teacher refer your child for assessment, perhaps because your child is not reading at grade level or seems bored with work, the psychologist works to determine the needs of your child and to help her meet those needs. The psychologist's assessment may also be to refer your child for further evaluation outside the arena of the school.

- **Consultation.** The school psychologist may work with you and the teacher to develop strategies to help your child when she is encountering problems ranging from difficulties with motivation to behavioral issues.

- **Testing.** Also related to assessment, the school psychologist administers any tests required to determine whether and in what ways your child qualifies for special education services. Likewise, the school may call upon the psychologist to review performance on state or national tests in conjunction with other tests, in order to get a complete picture of your child's special needs.

- **Crisis response.** Should any traumatic event occur at your child's school or in the life of any of the school's students, the psychologist will play a key role in the school's planning and response.

School psychologists are highly trained in both psychology and education, completing a minimum of a post-master's degree program that includes a year-long internship. In addition, they must be certified or licensed by the state in which they work.

When are times your child may need to speak with a school counselor?

Counselors work with the entire school population on a variety of issues relating to academic, personal, and social development. Your child may need to speak to the school counselor if he is:

- dealing with the death of a family member or a pet
- having a hard time concentrating in class because of difficulties with friends, cliques, bullying, or other social issues
- worried or stressed about an upcoming test, a home situation, or another concern that is interfering with his schoolwork
- involved in a behavioral or discipline situation

At times like these, the school counselor can be a great resource, either by being there for a half-hour chat or by providing ongoing consultation. School counselors also assist students with solving problems concerning course selection and scheduling. For example, if your middle school child has taken all the Spanish he can and needs to go to the local high school for the next level, the school counselor will be the person to arrange that.

In addition to providing guidance for individual students, school counselors may coordinate character education programs, friendship groups, and new student meetings and provide information on health issues and referrals to community services. Many parents and students have found their school counselor to be an invaluable friend, providing information on a variety of topics, from adjusting to school to improving study skills to planning for post-secondary school and a career. Parents know their children best, but the school counselor can help you better understand your child as a student.

School counselors are professional educators with a mental health perspective. Although not certified psychologists, they are trained in psychology. To become a counselor, most states require an individual to have a teaching degree in addition to a master's degree in school counseling, counselor education, or counseling psychology.

What do resource and curriculum specialists do?

In the course of her elementary and middle school career, your child may be referred to a resource teacher or curriculum specialist. School districts employ specialists with expertise in particular areas whose job is to diagnose and work with students who have special needs (such as students with learning difficulties or gifted students), to assist teachers with strategies to help those students, and to advise administrators on how to implement new state standards. Frequently, curriculum specialists split their time among the various schools in the district. They can serve as a resource in many areas but are most often available to deal with the following issues:

- **Speech and language.** Schools are required to provide help for any student with a documented problem in speech and language. Your child can be referred by her teacher or by you. If a teacher refers your child for speech and language evaluation or therapy, you will be notified.

- **Reading.** Even though elementary school teachers are typically reading teachers as well, most districts have a designated reading specialist who is qualified to do in-depth diagnostic screening if a child is having reading difficulties. The same specialist also may work individually or in small groups with students who need extra help with reading.

- **Special education.** Most schools provide access to at least one special educator in order to teach the children who qualify for these services and to assist teachers who have special education students in their regular classrooms. This specialist is generally part of a school's IEP or child study team. (See Chapter 11 for more on special education.)

What other school personnel can you turn to for help?

Here's a brief introduction to some of the other school personnel you may run into at your child's school and what their responsibilities are:

The building services manager, in accordance with sanitary, safety, and operating standards, manages and maintains the school facility: all the building operations, property, and schoolgrounds.

The media specialist, often with the help of a media assistant, administers the school's library media program, filters and researches online databases, and teaches students how to use the media center, conduct research, and use technology. The job of the media specialist (once known as the school librarian) has changed radically since the advent of computers and Internet services and includes spending time online gathering useful information to help enhance students' curriculum. Parents also can get reading lists from the media specialist and can access various databases, such as cyber-encyclopedias, through the school media center.

The paraeducator works under the supervision of the teacher and is an invaluable assistant in the classroom. In general, paraeducators work in conjunction with teachers to help deliver classroom instruction and to ensure that individual student needs are being met. They might also be called educational or instructional aides, classroom assistants, or paraprofessionals.

The school administrative secretary (or administrative assistant) is key to the smooth operation of the school. This professional supervises the work of a school's main office and provides primary office support for the principal. The secretary also provides parents and visitors with information on school procedures and policies.

Parents often wish to contact **the school bus driver,** who may or may not be an employee of the school. Many school districts run their own buses, but some outsource this service to independent companies. If there's a problem on the bus, it's important to call the school directly and speak to the principal or assistant principal. If your child has left something on the bus, someone at the school or at the bus company may be able to help you track it down. If you don't know who to call, contact the administrative assistant at your child's school to find out.

Where can you find out more?

On pages 175–177 you will find detailed resources related to special education. Check out the following organizations to learn more about specialized school personnel:

American School Counselor Association (ASCA)
1101 King Street, Suite 625
Alexandria, VA 22314
800-306-4722
www.schoolcounselor.org

This organization provides numerous helpful resources for parents, including "The Role of the School Counselor" and "Back-to-School Tips."

National Association of School Nurses (NASN)
8484 Georgia Avenue, Suite 420
Silver Spring, MD 20910
866-627-6767
www.nasn.org

National Association of School Psychologists (NASP)
4340 East-West Highway, Suite 402
Bethesda, MD 20814
866-331-6277
www.nasponline.org

IN CLOSING

The poet W.B. Yeats said it best: "Education is not filling a bucket, but lighting a fire." I was drawn to teaching because I knew from my experience as a student at Torquay Girls' High School in England that schools can be wondrous and exciting places. I still remember thrilling to the sound of Miss Russell, my fifth-form Shakespeare teacher, as she brought to life King Lear's sorrow at the death of his beloved daughter, Cordelia. Back then, I made it my goal to one day inspire my own students in the same way.

After being involved in classrooms for over twenty-five years, I continue to cherish those early memories, and I hope that I have been able to make a difference in the lives of some of my students in the way Miss Russell made a difference in mine. Over the years I have also learned that the give-and-take of teaching is much more complex than I realized as a high school student. My best teaching days are those where my students and I learn together—they from me, I from them.

As a teacher and parent, I wrote this book knowing that the more parents are informed about the workings of their child's school, the more they will benefit from their interactions with the school, its teachers, and its administration. I hope that this book will help you discover that schools are joyful and inspiring environments and that being involved in your child's education not only helps your child, but also helps to rekindle the fire of learning in you.

EDU-SPEAK
A Glossary of Terms

Here is a guide to the ever-evolving lingo of the classroom.

ability grouping Separation of students into groups based on ability, often used synonymously with the term *tracking*.

acceptable use policy (AUP) Policy to inform students about the appropriate use of the Internet and the consequences for failure to act responsibly when using online resources.

accountability Policy that holds districts, schools, or students responsible for their performance. Accountability often involves rating schools, districts, or students based on test scores or other assessments and rewarding or imposing sanctions based on improvement over time.

adequate yearly progress (AYP) Formula for telling whether schools are meeting their goals for improvement as determined by the state. The purpose of measuring AYP is to hold the public education system accountable for teaching *all* students, as required under the No Child Left Behind Act (NCLB).

adequacy School funding approach built on the idea that schools should have enough (adequate) money for students to achieve their state's educational goals.

alternative schools Schools designed to provide nurturing environments for students at risk of school failure.

assessment Measurement of a student's skills or knowledge in a subject area.

attention deficit disorder/attention deficit hyperactivity disorder (ADD/ADHD) Condition characterized by the inability to concentrate, impulsivity, inattention, and/or hyperactivity.

authentic assessment Gauging of students' knowledge in ways other than by the use of conventional standardized tests. Examples include hands-on demonstrations of knowledge like writing an essay, conducting a science experiment, or creating portfolios. Also called alternative or performance assessment.

average daily attendance (ADA) Average number of students who attend a school over the course of the year. ADA is determined by the total number of days of student attendance divided by the total number of days in the regular school year.

bilingual education Education program for nonnative English speakers. Students spend part of the school day receiving instruction in their native language, with a goal of moving them into mainstream English classes, normally within two or three years.

charter schools Publicly funded schools that have been exempted from certain rules and regulations that apply to other public schools. In exchange for these exemptions, they are accountable for producing specific results outlined in the schools' charters.

child study team Group of people who determine whether a student is eligible for special education services, usually the teacher, a counselor or psychologist, the principal, the school nurse, and any other relevant specialists. Also known as student study team, school screening committee, or other names.

Children's Internet Protection Act (CIPA) Federal law mandating that any school receiving discounted rates for Internet access, Internet service, or internal connections must develop an Internet safety policy and use protection measures that block or filter Internet access to material that is harmful to minors.

conflict mediation System of resolving disputes through talking. Many schools use variations of this as a way of solving problems. The goal of conflict mediation is to help students communicate clearly, understand one another, and focus on how they can best work together.

cooperative learning Teaching method in which students of varying abilities and interests work together in small groups on a specific task or project. Students complete assignments together and receive a common grade.

crisis management plan School's plan for managing an emergency such as a bomb threat, a fire, or natural disaster. A trained crisis management team—school administrators and other critical staff—implements the crisis management plan. As part of this plan, schools are required to conduct fire safety and emergency preparedness drills.

criterion-referenced tests (CRT) Tests that measure a student's performance against a set body of content. Tests that match state standards (standards-based tests) are criterion-referenced tests: they are designed to measure how well a child has learned a specific body of knowledge and skills.

curriculum Subject matter that teachers and students cover in class, as well as the educational ends sought for students, usually described as goals or objectives.

district superintendent Administrator who leads the implementation of district goals and manages the day-to-day operations of the school district.

due process Legal concept ensuring that the government will respect *all* of a person's legal rights instead of just some or most of them. For example, due process means that children undergoing suspension have the right to know the school's rules ahead of time, to receive adequate notice of the charges, and to challenge the charges.

education foundation Nonprofit, community-based group that raises money for schools. Most education foundations operate independently from the school districts they support.

ELL (English language learner) Student who is still learning English as a new language. Also called LEP (limited-English proficient) and EL (English learner).

emergency credential License to teach that bypasses state licensing requirements. Sometimes extended because of critical teacher shortage, these credentials are often granted to individuals to teach in high-need subject areas, such as mathematics, science, or special education, or for high-need geographic areas. Also called temporary credential.

enrichment program Education designed to supplement the regular academic curriculum.

enrollment Count of the students enrolled in each school and district on a given day, usually in October.

equity School funding approach built on the idea that states are required to distribute resources fairly to all students no matter where they live.

ESOL (English for speakers of other languages) Classes for eligible English language learners. Also known as ESL (English as a second language) and ELD (English language development).

free appropriate public education (FAPE) Education guaranteed for any student attending a school that receives public funds. For students with disabilities, this means they may be eligible for special-needs education services that are consistent with a child's Individualized Education Program (IEP) at no additional cost to the parents.

gifted Term describing young people who give evidence of high achievement capability in areas such as intellectual, creative, artistic, or leadership capacity, or in specific academic fields, and who need services and activities not ordinarily provided by the school in order to fully develop those capabilities.

high-stakes tests Tests used by districts and states to make important decisions that affect an individual child or a school. Scores may be used to determine a child's future, such as whether a student graduates or continues on to the next grade, or a school's future, such as replacing the administration and much of the staff.

IEP team Group of people who come together to create an Individualized Education Program (IEP), usually the student's classroom teacher, a school counselor or psychologist, the resource specialist, the principal or assistant principal, and the child's parents or legal guardians.

inclusion Educational practice based on the philosophy that all children, regardless of their special needs, can and should be educated together in the same classroom. This means that students who are in the special education program enroll in general education classes, while they continue to receive support from the special education teacher.

independent schools Private, nonprofit schools governed by elected boards of trustees that are funded through tuition payments, charitable contributions, and endowments.

Individualized Education Program (IEP) Education plan prepared for each public school child who receives special education and related services. Reviewed annually, with a complete reevaluation every three years, the IEP is a legal document that must be adhered to.

Individuals with Disabilities Education Act (IDEA) The main federal program authorizing state and local aid for special education services for children with disabilities, including students with learning disabilities.

IQ (intelligence quotient) Measure of a person's capacity or aptitude for learning. IQ tests measure one facet of intelligence as displayed in verbal and logical thinking; IQ scores alone do not determine a student's academic needs.

learning disability Life-long disorder affecting how individuals with normal or above-average intelligence store, process, or produce information. A learning disability usually reveals itself in a discrepancy between intelligence and academic achievement.

magnet schools Publicly funded special-focus schools designed to bring in students from outside the local neighborhood to reduce or eliminate racial imbalance. They offer programs designed for students with special abilities, interests, or needs.

mainstreaming Process of integrating students with special needs into regular school classes.

media specialist Specialist who administers the school's library media program, filters and researches online databases, and teaches students how to use the media center, conduct research, and use technology.

multimedia Use of multiple media types to convey information, like text along with audio, graphics, and animation, which may be packaged on a CD-ROM and include links to the Internet.

narrative report card Report that contains written comments by a child's teacher and conveys more detailed information than is possible with a letter or number grade alone.

National Assessment of Educational Progress (NAEP) Federal test that provides information about the educational progress of students in the United States and in specific geographic regions in the country. Also called "The Nation's Report Card," NAEP administers reading and math tests every two years and tests other subjects in alternate years.

No Child Left Behind Act (NCLB) Most recent reauthorization of the federal government's comprehensive K–12 program, the Elementary and Secondary Education Act (ESEA), which began in 1965. NCLB redefines the federal role in K–12 education in an effort to close the achievement gap between disadvantaged children and their peers. It is based on four principles: stronger accountability for results, increased flexibility and local control, expanded options for parents, and an emphasis on teaching methods that have been proven to work.

norm-referenced tests Tests that compare the performance of individual test takers to that of a nationally representative group of test takers. For example, a student in the fourth grade is compared to other fourth graders taking the same test.

open enrollment Policy that allows parents to choose where their child attends school as opposed to being assigned to a school based on where the child lives.

paraeducator Trained assistant who works with teachers to help deliver classroom instruction and to ensure that individual student needs are being met. Also called educational or instructional aide, classroom assistant, or paraprofessional.

Parent Teacher Association (PTA) Largest volunteer child advocacy organization in the U.S. Local PTA groups pay dues to the state and national organization and in return receive member benefits and a voice in the operations of the larger organization.

Parent Teacher Organization (PTO) Umbrella organization that represents parent-teacher groups that are independent of the PTA. Groups may take other names such as PCC (Parent Communication Council), PTG (Parent-Teacher Group), and HAS (Home and School Association). These are most often single-school groups operating under their own bylaws and working for their individual school or community.

peer counselors Student volunteers, recommended by the faculty, who are trained to listen and help other students who are experiencing some difficulty. Training is usually conducted by the school counselors, who also run the program.

peer helpers Students who help other students in academic or social areas. Peer helpers may be paired with new students to help them adjust to the new environment or may serve as tutors for younger students.

portfolio Systematic collection of a student's work that may be used as part of a standardized assessment system or by an individual teacher as part of ongoing classroom grading. It generally includes some sort of self-reflection by the student.

private schools Term describing nonpublic schools, either religious or independent, typically nonprofit and tuition-based.

proprietary schools Private schools that are run for profit, like a business.

pull-out program Program that removes a student from the regular classroom setting for one or more sessions a week in order to see an education specialist.

religious schools Private schools established and operated by religious organizations. Also called parochial schools.

Response to Intervention (RTI) Multi-stage process that allows states and school districts to provide services and interventions at increasing levels of intensity to students who struggle with learning. Student progress is closely monitored at each stage. Results of monitoring are used to make decisions about the need for further research-based instruction and/or intervention in general education, in special education, or both.

rubric A set of scoring criteria for a project or assignment that the student knows ahead of time. Rubrics can help students understand the strengths and weaknesses of their work better than they could with letter grades alone.

Section 504 Civil rights law, part of the Rehabilitation Act of 1973, that prohibits programs receiving federal funding from discriminating on the basis of disabling conditions. Section 504 does not require a child to be identified as needing special education under IDEA to qualify, and it is generally less sweeping than special education. Unlike IDEA, this statute does not require that the federal government provide additional funding for students identified with special needs.

social promotion Practice of automatically passing students to the next grade at the end of the year regardless of whether they have met performance standards and academic requirements for promotion.

special education Education designed to serve children with mental and physical disabilities. These children are entitled to Individualized Education Programs (IEPs) that spell out the services they need to reach their educational goals, ranging from speech therapy to math tutoring.

standardized tests Assessments developed using standard procedures and administered and scored in a consistent manner for all test takers. The standardization of tests helps ensure that the test scores are comparable and as unbiased as possible.

standards Clear statements about what students should know and be able to do in certain subject areas and at certain stages in their education. Standards can be academic, content, or performance based.

Title I Program evolved from the Elementary and Secondary Education Act of 1965 (ESEA) that provides extra resources to schools and school districts with the highest concentrations of poverty.

twice-exceptional Term describing young people who are designated as both gifted and having learning or attention difficulties.

vouchers Certificates that allow parents to use public funds for their children's education at a school of their choice—often a private school.

Webmaster Person responsible for designing, developing and maintaining a Web site. Also called Internet director.

zero tolerance Policy under which particular types of misconduct are simply not tolerated and specific consequences or interventions are established and applied in all cases.

INDEX

ABOUT THE AUTHOR

An award-winning teacher and writer, Judy Molland has keenly observed and actively participated in the world of education for over twenty-five years, both in the United States and in her native England. She holds a B.A. Honors degree from the University of Hull, England, and a Diploma in Education from the University of London Institute of Education. Beginning her career as a classroom teacher, a role from which she continues to derive great satisfaction, she has also been writing about education for over ten years. Since 1988, Judy has been Contributing Education Editor for Dominion Parenting Media, the largest syndicate of parenting magazines in the U.S., and she has numerous articles featured on Parenthood.com. Her writing has also appeared in several other publications including *Parents*, *Instructor*, *New York Newsday*, *Metro Kids*, and *Chicago Parent*. Passionate about education, she loves pursuing her dual career of teacher/writer.

Judy began her teaching career at Rotherhithe Junior School in London, England. Her first position in the U.S. was with the Yellow Brick Road Kindergarten School in Berkeley, California, and she has since taught at all grade levels from fourth to twelfth, in both the public and the private arena, in places as diverse as Simi Valley, California; Brooklyn, New York; and Rockville, Maryland. She currently teaches in Belmont, California. Judy resides in Redwood City, California, with her husband.

Fast, Friendly, and Easy to Use

www.freespirit.com